ITIL® V3 Foundation Complete Certification Kit - Study Guide

Foreword

As an education and training organization within the IT Service Management (ITSM) industry, we have been impressed by the positive changes introduced by the refresh of ITIL® in July 2007. The evolution of the core principles and practices provided by the framework provides the more holistic guidance needed for an industry that continues to mature and develop at a rapid pace. We recognize however, that many organizations and individuals who had previously struggled with their adoption of the framework will continue to find challenges in 'implementing' ITIL® as part of their approach for governance of IT Service Management practices. In light of this, one of our primary goals is to provide the quality education and support materials needed to enable the understanding and application of the ITIL® framework in a wide-range of contexts.

This comprehensive book is designed to complement the indepth accredited eLearn ITIL® Foundation course provided by The Art of Service. The interactive eLearn course uses a combination of narrated PowerPoint presentations with flat text supplements and multiple choice assessments. This book value adds the eLearn course by providing additional text and real life examples to further cement your knowledge. Your learning and understanding will be maximized by combining these two study resources, which will ultimately prepare you for the APMG ITIL® Foundation certification exam.

We hope you find this book to be a useful tool in your educational library and wish you well in you IT Service Management career!

The Art of Service

How to access the associated eLearning Program:

1. Direct your browser to: www.theartofservice.org
2. Click 'login' (found at the top right of the page)
3. Click 'Create New Account'
4. Follow the instructions to create a new account. You will need a valid email address to confirm your account creation. If you do not receive the confirmation email check that it has not been automatically moved to a Junk Mail or Spam folder.
5. Once your account has been confirmed, email your User-ID for your new account to elearningbook@theartofservice.com .
6. We will add your account to the Foundation eLearning Program and let you know how to access the program from now on.

Minimum system requirements for accessing the eLearning Program:

Processor	: Pentium III (600 MHz) or higher
RAM	: 128MB (256MB recommended)
OS	: Windows 98, NT, 2000, ME, XP, 2003, Mac OSX
Browser	: Internet Explorer 5.x or higher (Cookies and JavaScript Enabled), Safari
Plug-Ins	: Macromedia Flash Player 8
Other Hardware	: 16-bit Sound Card, Mouse, Speakers or headphones
Display Settings	: 1024x768 pixels
Internet Connection	: Due to multimedia content of the site, a minimum connection speed of 256kbs is recommended. If you are behind a firewall and are facing problems in accessing the course or the learning portal, please contact your network administrator for help

If you are experiencing difficulties with the Flash Presentations within the eLearning Programs please make sure that:

1) You have the latest version of Flash Player installed, by visiting
http://www.adobe.com/shockwave/download/download.cgi?P1_Prod_Version=ShockwaveFlash

2) You check that your security settings in your web browser don't prevent these flash modules playing. There is support for these issues at the following page:
http://kb.adobe.com/selfservice/viewContent.do?externalId=tn_19166&sliceId=2#no_content

Contents

1 Introduction

The term IT Service Management (ITSM) is used in many ways by different management frameworks and organizations seeking governance and increased maturity of their IT organization. Standard elements for most definitions of ITSM include:

- Description of the **processes** required to deliver and support IT Services for customers.
- The purpose primarily being to deliver and support the **technology or products** needed by the business to meet key organizational objectives or goals.
- Definition of roles and responsibilities for the **people** involved including IT staff, customers and other stakeholders involved.
- The management of **external suppliers (partners)** involved in the delivery and support of the technology and products being delivered and supported by IT.

The combination of these elements provide the capabilities required for an IT organization to deliver and support quality IT Services that meet specific business needs and requirements.

The official ITIL® definition of IT Service Management is found within the Service Design book on page 11, describing ITSM as *"A set of specialized organizational capabilities for providing value to customers in the form of services"*.

1.1 The Four Perspectives (Attributes) of ITSM

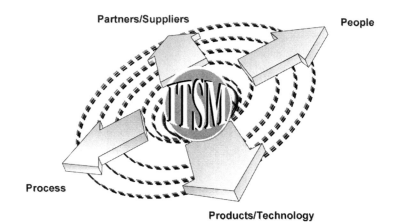

Figure 1.A – Four Perspectives (Attributes) of ITSM

There are four perspectives ("4P's") or attributes to explain the concept of ITSM.

- **Partners/Suppliers Perspective:**
Takes into account the importance of Partner and External Supplier relationships and how they contribute to Service Delivery.
- **People Perspective:**
Concerned with the "soft" side: IT staff, customers and other stakeholders. E.g. Do staff have the correct skills and knowledge to perform their roles?
- **Products/Technology Perspective:**
Takes into account IT services, hardware & software, budgets, tools.
- **Process Perspective:**
Relates the end to end delivery of service based on process flows.

Quality IT Service Management ensures that all of these four perspectives are taken into account as part of the continual improvement of the IT organization.

1.2 Benefits of ITSM

While the benefits of applying IT Service Management practices vary depending on the organization's needs, some typical benefits include:
- improved quality service provision
- cost justifiable service quality
- services that meet business, Customer and User demands
- integrated centralized processes
- everyone knows their role and knows their responsibilities in service provision
- learning from previous experience
- demonstrable performance indicators

1.3 Business and IT Alignment

A central concept to keep in mind when discussing the benefits of IT Service Management is the goal of business and IT alignment. When staff members of an IT organization have an internal focus on the technology being delivered and supported, they lose sight of the actual purpose and benefit that their efforts deliver to the business. A way in which to communicate how IT supports the business is using the following Figure demonstrating business and IT alignment.

Figure 1.B below divides an organization into a number of supporting layers that work towards meeting a number of organizational goals. These layers are communicated by the following:

1. **Organization** (What are the key goals for the organization?)
2. **CORE Business Processes** (These business processes enable the objectives above to be met)
3. **IT Service Organization** (What IT Services are required to enable the effective and efficient execution of the business processes above?)
4. **IT Service Management** (The focus here is on the ITIL® processes required for quality delivery and support of the IT Services above)
5. **IT Technical Activities** (The actual technical activities required as part of the execution of the ITIL® processes above. These are technology specific and as such not the focus of ITIL® or this document.

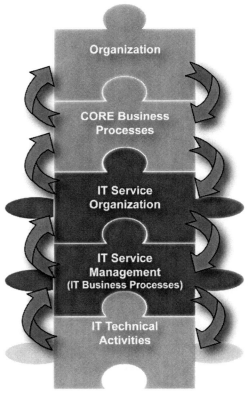

Figure 1.B – Business and IT Alignment

Example to illustrate business and IT alignment:
Business: A fashion store

What are some of your organization's objectives or strategic goals?
We want to make a lot of money $$$!
We want to have a good image and reputation.

What Business Processes aide in achieving those objectives?
Retail, marketing, buying, procurement, HR etc.

What IT Services are these business processes dependent on?
Web site, email, automatic procurement system for buying products, Point of Sale Services

We have ITSM in order to make sure the IT Services are:
What we need (Service Level Management, Capacity Management etc)
Available when we need it (Availability MGT, Incident MGT etc.)
Provisioned cost-effectively (Financial MGT, Service Level MGT)

If we don't manage the IT Services appropriately we cannot rely on these services to be available when we need. If this occurs we cannot adequately support our business processes effectively and efficiently. And therefore we cannot meet or support our overall organization's objectives!!!

1.4 What is ITIL®?

ITIL® stands for the Information Technology Infrastructure Library. ITIL® is the international de facto management framework describing "best practices" for IT Service Management. The ITIL® framework evolved from the UK government's efforts during the 1980s to document how successful organizations approached service management. By the early 1990s they had produced a large collection of books documenting the "best practices" for IT Service Management. This library was eventually entitled the IT Infrastructure Library. The Office of Government Commerce in the UK continues to operate as the trademark owner of ITIL®.

ITL has gone through several evolutions and was most recently refreshed with the release of version 3 in 2007. Through these evolutions the scope of practices documented has increased in order to stay current with the continued maturity of the IT industry and meet the needs and requirements of the ITSM professional community.

ITL is only one of many sources for best practices, including those documented by:
- **Public frameworks** (ITIL®, COBIT, CMMI etc.)
- **Standards** (ISO 20 000, BS 15 000)
- **Proprietary knowledge of organizations and individuals**

Generally best practices are those formalized as a result of being **successful in wide-industry use.**

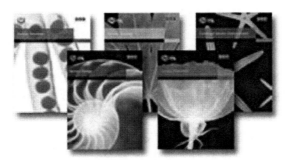

Five volumes make up the IT Infrastructure Library (Version 3).
- Service Strategy
- Service Design
- Service Transition
- Service Operation
- Continual Service Improvement

2 Common Terminology

Critical to our ability to participate with and apply the concepts from the ITIL® framework is the need to be able to speak a common language with other IT staff, customers, end-users and other involved stakeholders. This next section documents the important common terminology that is used throughout the ITIL® framework.

Terminology	Explanations
IT Service Management:	A set of specialized organizational capabilities for providing value to customers in the form of services.
Capabilities:	The ability of an organization, person, process, application, CI or IT service to carry out an activity. • The functions and processes utilized to manage services. • Capabilities are intangible assets of an organization and cannot be purchased, but must be developed and matured over time. • *The ITSM set of organizational capabilities aims to enable the effective and efficient delivery of services to customers.*
Resources:	A generic term that includes IT Infrastructure, people, money or anything else that might help to deliver an IT service. Resources are also considered to be tangible assets of an organization.
Process:	A set of *coordinated activities* combining and implementing resources and capabilities in order to produce an outcome and *provide value to customers or stakeholders.* • Processes are *strategic assets* when they create competitive advantage and market differentiation. • Processes *may* define roles, responsibilities, tools, management controls, policies, standards, guidelines, activities and work instructions if they are needed.

Functions:	A team or group of *people* and the tools they use to carry out one or more Processes or Activities. Functions provide units of organization responsible for specific outcomes. *ITIL® Functions covered include:*
	• Service Desk
	• Technical Management
	• Application Management
	• IT Operations Management

RACI Model: A technique used to define roles and responsibilities of people or groups in relation to processes and activities.

R – Responsibility (actually does the work for that activity but reports to the function or position that has an "A" against it).

A – Accountability (is made accountable for ensuring that the action takes place, even if they might not do it themselves).

C – Consult (advice/ guidance / information can be gained from this function or position prior to the action taking place).

I – Inform (the function or position that is told about the event after it has happened). **Refer to Figure 2.A***

Service: A means of delivering value to Customers by facilitating outcomes customers want to achieve without the ownership of specific costs or risks

Process Owner: The person responsible for ensuring that the process is fit for the desired purpose and is accountable for the outputs of that process.
Example: The owner for the Availability Management Process

Service Owner: The person who is accountable for the delivery of a specific IT Service. They are responsible for continual improvement and management of change affecting Services under their care.
Example: The owner of the Payroll Service

Process Manager: The person responsible for the operational management of a process. There may be several Managers for the one process. They report to the Process Owner.

Internal Service Providers: An internal service provider that is embedded within a business unit. E.g. one IT organization within each of the business units. The key factor is that the *IT Services provide a source of competitive advantage* in the market space the business exists in.

Shared Service Providers: An internal service provider that provides shared IT service to more than 1 business unit eg: one IT organization to service all businesses in a umbrella organization. IT Services typically don't provide a source of competitive advantage, but instead *support effective and efficient business processes.*

External Service Providers: Service provider that provides IT services to external customers. i.e. outsourcing

Business Case A decision support and planning tool that projects the likely consequences of a business action. It provides justification for a significant item of expenditure. Includes information about costs, benefits, options, issues, risks and possible problems.

RACI Model

	Service Desk	Desktop	Applications	Operations Manager
Logging	RACI	-	-	CI
Classification	RACI	RCI	-	CI
Investigation	ACI	RCI	RCI	CI

Figure 2.A – The RACI Model:

A RACI Model is used to define the roles and responsibilities of various Functions in relation to the activities of Incident Management.

General Rules:
Only 1 "A" per Row (ensures accountability, more than one "A" would confuse this)
At least 1 "R" per Row (shows that actions are taking place)

3 The Service Lifecycle_____

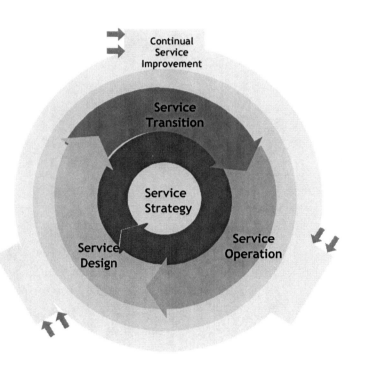

Figure 3.A – ITIL® Service Lifecycle Model

(Acknowledgement – OGC)

Lifecycle: *The natural process of stages that an organism or inanimate object goes through as it matures. For example, human stages are birth, infant, toddler, kid, pre-teen, teenager, young adult, adult and death.*

The concept of the **Service Lifecycle** is fundamental to the refresh of ITIL® for Version 3. Previously, much of the focus of ITIL® was on the **processes** required to design, deliver and support services for customers.

As a result of this previous focus on processes, Version 2 of the ITIL® Framework provided best practices for ITSM based around the *how* questions. These included:
- How should we design for availability, capacity and continuity of services?
- How can we respond to and manage incidents, problems and known errors?

As Version 3 now maintains a holistic view covering the entire lifecycle of a service, no longer does ITIL® just answer the how questions, but also *why?*
- Why does a customer need this service?
- Why should the customer purchase services from us?
- Why should we provide (x) levels of availability, capacity and continuity?

By first asking these questions it enables a service provider to provide overall **strategic objectives** for the IT organization, which will then be used to direct *how* services are **designed, transitioned, supported and improved** in order to deliver maximum value to customers and stakeholders.

The ultimate success of service management is indicated by the strength of the relationship between customers and service providers. The 5 phases of the Service Lifecycle provide the necessary guidance to achieve this success. Together they provide a body of knowledge and set of good practices for successful service management.

This end-to-end view of how IT should be integrated with business strategy is at the heart of ITIL®'s five core volumes (books).

3.1 Mapping the Concepts of ITIL® to the Service Lifecycle

There has been much debate as to exactly how many processes exist within Version 3 of ITIL®. Questions asked include:
- What exactly constitutes a process?
- Shouldn't some processes be defined as functions?
- Why has x process been left out?

In developing this material we have based our definitions of processes and functions and where they fit on the guidance provided by the ITIL® Foundation syllabus by EXIN International. Figure 3.B demonstrates the processes and functions of ITIL® in relation to the 5 Service Lifecycle Phases. It also demonstrates the increased scope now covered by ITIL® over the previous version.

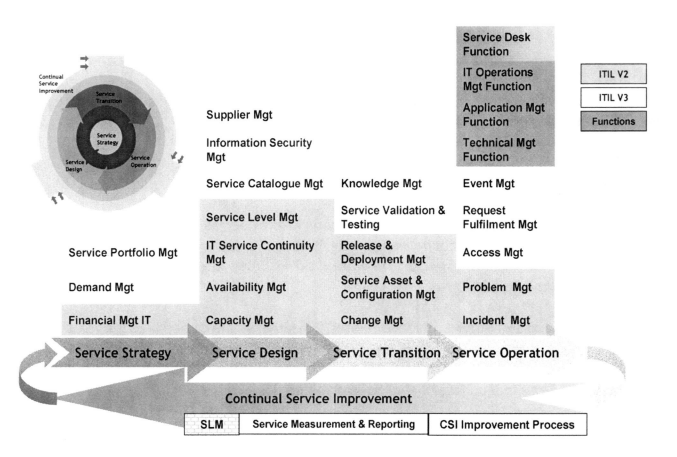

Figure 3.B – The Major Concepts of ITIL®

NOTES:

- The Service Lifecycle phases (and ITIL® books) are shown through the arrows at the bottom.
- The concepts in light shading are the V2 ITIL® concepts.
- The concepts not shaded are the new ITIL® V3 concepts.
- The concepts in dark shading are Functions.
- Although Service Level Management officially sits in the Service Design book, it plays a very important role in the Continual Service Improvement phase, and therefore could also fit in the CSI book as a process.

3.2 How does the Service Lifecycle work?

Although there are 5 phases throughout the Lifecycle, they are not separate, nor are the phases necessarily carried out in a particular order. The whole ethos of the Service Lifecycle approach is that each phase will affect the other, creating a continuous cycle. For this to work successfully, the Continuous Service Improvement (CSI) phase is incorporated throughout all of the other phases. Figure 3.C demonstrates some the key outputs from each of the Service Lifecycle Phases.

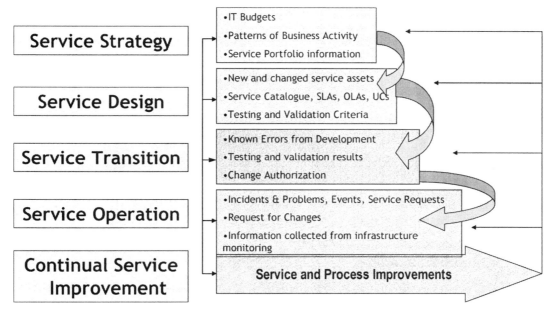

Figure 3.C – How does the Service Lifecycle Work?

It is important to note that most of the processes defined do not get executed within only one lifecycle phase. As an example we will look at the process of **Availability Management** and where some activities will get executed throughout Service Lifecycle.

Service Design Phase: Designs the infrastructure, processes and support mechanisms needed to meet the Availability requirements of the customer.

Service Transition Phase: Validates that the Service meets the functional and technical fitness criteria to justify release to the customer.

Service Operation Phase: Monitors the ongoing Availability being provided. During this phase we also manage and resolve incidents that affect Service Availability.

4 Service Strategy_____

What is strategy?

The term strategy was traditionally used in the military world, where strategy defined the distribution and application of military resources in order to meet the objectives of a plan.

Strategy in the context of Service Management is used by Service Providers to:

- **Attain Market focus** – deciding where and how to compete
- **Distinguish capabilities** – develop service assets that the business appreciates

The processes found within the Service Strategy lifecycle phase are:

- Financial Management for IT Services
- Service Portfolio Management
- Demand Management

4.1 Objectives

The primary objectives of Service Strategy are to:

- Design, develop and implement service management as a strategic asset and assisting growth of the organization.
- Develop the IT organization's capability to manage the costs and risks associated with their service portfolios.
- Define the strategic objectives of the IT organization.

By achieving these objectives it will ensure that the IT organization has a clear understanding of how it can better support business growth, efficiency improvements or other strategies that wish to be realized.

KEY ROLE: To stop and think about WHY something has to be done, before thinking HOW.

4.2 Major Concepts

4.2.1 Creating Service Value

One of the major concepts developed within the Service Strategy phase is determining how to create Service value. This ensures that before rushing out to determine how to design a Service, we stop and ask two important questions:

- Why does the customer need this Service?
- Why should the customer purchase it from us?

To answer these questions we will look at the two factors that combine to create value in IT Services.

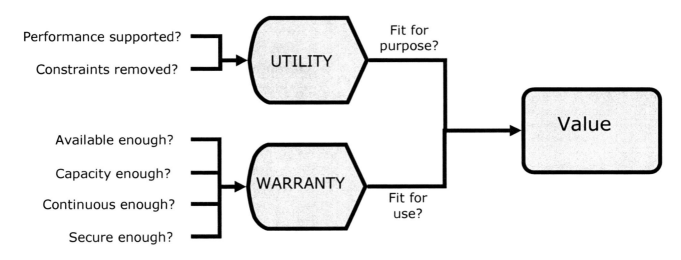

Figure 4.A – Creating Service Value

Service Warranty + Service Utility = Service Value

Service Utility defines the functionality of an IT Service from the customer's perspective (i.e.: what the service does)

Service Warranty for a service provides the customer a level of reassurance and guarantee to meet agreed requirements. (Example attributes: Availability, capacity, continuity, security etc)

These two factors will be communicated via the Service Package produced by the IT organization for use by customers. By doing this it clearly communicates the value offered so that customers can make an informed decision whether to acquire the Service for use.

4.2.2 Service Packages and Service Level Packages

To discuss Service Packages, Service Level Packages and how they are used to offer choice and value to customers, we're going to use the example of the packages made available by typical Internet Service Providers (ISPs).

As customers, we have a wide range of choice when looking for an ISP to provide broadband internet. So as a result ISPs do need to work hard to attract customers by communicating the value that they provide through their offerings. They also need to offer a wide range of choice for customers, who have varying requirements and needs for their broadband internet service.

Service Packages:

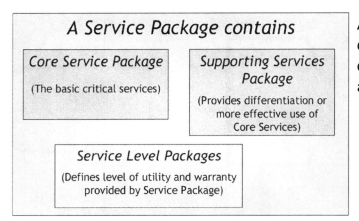

A **Service Package** provides a detailed description of a service available to be delivered to Customers. The contents of a Service Package includes:
- The core services provided
- Any supporting services provided (often the excitement factors)
- The Service Level Package (see next page)

Service Level Packages:

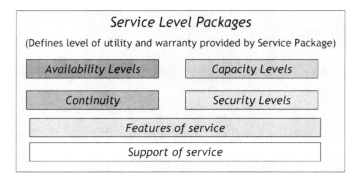

Service Level Packages are effective in developing service packages with levels of utility and warranty appropriate to the customer's needs and in a cost-effective way.
- Availability Levels
- Continuity (e.g. Disaster Recovery)
- Capacity Levels (inc. performance)
- Security Levels

So for our ISP example, we can define a Service Package in the following way:

Figure 4.B – Service Package Example (ISP)

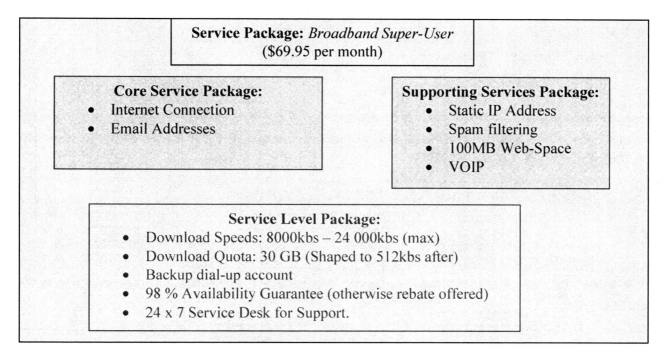

Most of the components of Service Packages and Service Level Packages are reusable components of the IT organization (many of which are services). Other components include software, hardware and other infrastructure elements. By providing Service Level Packages in this way it reduces the cost and complexity of providing services while maintaining high levels of customer satisfaction. In our example above, the ISP can easily create multiple Service Packages with varying levels of Utility and Warranty provided in order to offer a wide range of choice to customers, and to distinguish themselves from their competition.

The use of Service Packages and Service Level Packages enables Service Providers to avoid a one-size fits all approach to IT Services.

4.3 Service Strategy Processes

The processes included in the Service Strategy lifecycle phase are:
- Financial Management for IT Services
- Service Portfolio Management
- Demand Management

These three processes work together to enable an IT organization to maximize the value of services being provided to customers and to provide the quality information required to make investment decisions regarding IT.

4.3.1 Financial Management for IT Services

GOAL: To provide cost effective stewardship of the IT assets and the financial resources used in providing IT services. This enables an organization to account fully for the spend on IT Services and to attribute these costs to the services delivered to the organization's customers.

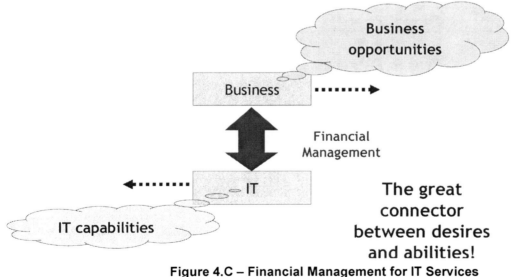

Figure 4.C – Financial Management for IT Services

Using Financial Management for IT (FMIT) to provide services with cost transparency (e.g. via service catalogue) clearly understood by the business and then rolled into the planning process for demand modeling and funding is a powerful benefit for the organization. It enables the best balance to be struck between the opportunities available for the business against the capabilities levels of the IT organization.

Activities

There are three fundamental activities for Financial Management for IT Services. These are:
1. Budgeting
2. IT Accounting
3. Charging.

1. **Budgeting:** Predicting the expected future requirements for funds to deliver the agreed upon services and monitoring adherence to the defined budgets. This ensures that the required resources to fund IT are made available and can improve the business case for IT projects and initiatives.

2. **IT Accounting:** Enables the IT organization to account fully for the way its money is spent. The definition of Cost Models can be used to identify costs by customer, by service, by activity or other logical groupings. IT Accounting supports more accurate Budgeting and ensures that any Charging method utilized is simple, fair and realistic.

3. **Charging: (optional activity)** Charging customers for their use of IT Services. Charging can be implemented in a number of ways in order to encourage more efficient use of IT resources. Notional charging is one option, in which the costs of providing Services to customers are communicated but no actual payment is required.

Other Terminology (Not Examined at a Foundation Level)

Terminology	Explanations
Cost Types:	These are higher level expenses identified such as hardware, software, people, accommodation, transfer and external costs.
Cost Elements:	The actual elements making up the cost types above. E.G. For the hardware cost type it would include the elements such as CPUs, Servers, Desktops etc.
Direct Costs:	Cost elements identified to be clearly attributed to only a single customer or service.
Indirect Costs:	Often known as overheads, these are costs that are shared across multiple customers or services, which have to be shared in a fair manner.
Cost Units:	A cost unit is the identified unit of consumption that is accounted for a particular service or service asset.

FMIT assists in the task of Service Valuation, which is used to help the business and the IT Service Provider agree on the value of the IT Service. It determines the balance demonstrating the total cost of providing an IT Service against the total value offered to the business by the Service.

Service Value for services is created by the combination of Service Utility and Service Warranty.

4.3.2 Service Portfolio Management

GOAL: To assist the IT organization in managing investments in service management across the enterprise and maximizing them for value.

A **Service Portfolio** describes provider's services in terms of business value. They include the complete set of services managed by a Service Provider. These portfolios are used to articulate business needs and the Service Provider's response to those needs. It is possible for a Service Provider to have multiple Service Portfolios depending on the customer groups that they support.

- Includes the complete set of services managed by a service Provider.
- Provides the information required to manage the entire lifecycle of all services.

3 Categories of services defined in Service Portfolio
- Service Pipeline (proposed or in development)
- Service Catalogue (Live or available for deployment)
- Retired Services (Decommissioned services)

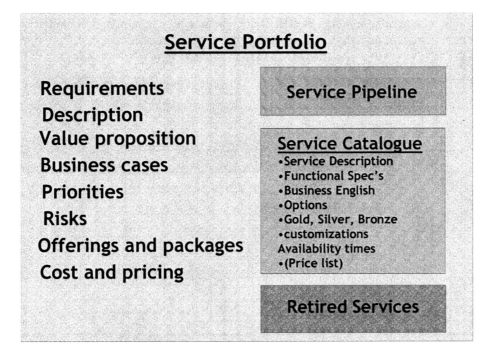

Figure 4.D – A Service Portfolio

Service Portfolios have a much larger scope than Service Catalogues, and is used to manage the lifecycle of all services in order to maximize the value of IT Service Management to the business.

The Portfolio should have the right mix of services in the pipeline and catalogue to secure the financial viability of the service provider. Just like a Financial Portfolio, we need to ensure the balance between risk and benefit provided by the Service Portfolio.

The Service Portfolio uses the above information to provide informed responses to the following strategic questions:

1. Why should a customer buy these services?
2. Why should they buy these services from us?
3. What are the pricing or chargeback models?
4. What are our strengths and weaknesses, priorities and risk?
5. How are resources and capabilities to be allocated?

Service Portfolio Management is a dynamic and ongoing process and includes the following methods:

Define: Used to validate portfolio data. It is the assessment of services investment in terms of potential benefits and the resources and capabilities required to provision and maintain them. This also enables the Service Provider to define what it can not do (due to maturity levels, capabilities, risks etc). Through this activity, the initial creation of the Service Portfolio begins.

Analyze: Maximize portfolio value, align and prioritize and balance supply and demand. This is where strategic intent is created. Questions asked here include:

- What are the long term goals of the service org?
- What services are required to meet those goals?
- What capabilities and resources are required to deliver and support those services?
- How will we get there?

Approve: Finalize proposed portfolio, authorize services and resources needed to deliver services.

Charter: Plans and tracks the progress of service investments across the portfolio and allocate the required resources. Used to schedule and manage the design, transition, change and retirement of services.

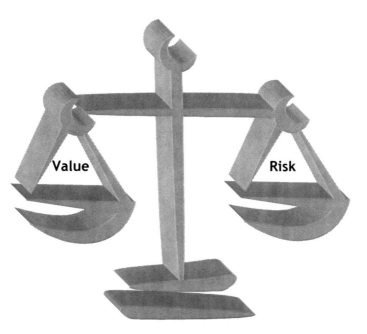

Figure 4.E – Balancing a Service Portfolio

Understanding their options helps senior executives to make informed investment decisions in service initiatives with appropriate levels of risks and rewards. These initiatives may cross business functions and may span short, medium and longer time frames.

Investment categories & Budget Allocations
Service Investments are split among 3 strategic categories:

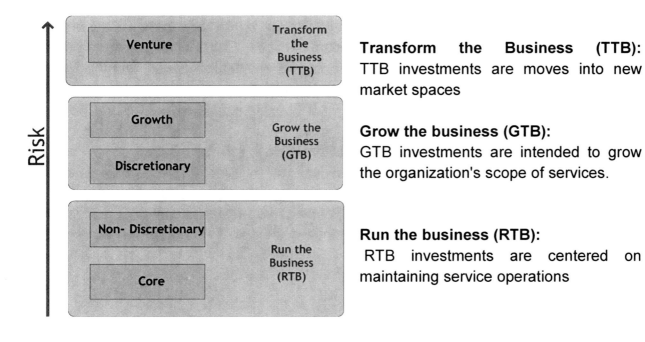

Transform the Business (TTB): TTB investments are moves into new market spaces

Grow the business (GTB): GTB investments are intended to grow the organization's scope of services.

Run the business (RTB): RTB investments are centered on maintaining service operations

The outcomes for existing services fall into 6 categories:

RENEW: These services meet functional fitness criteria, but fail technical fitness.

REPLACE: These services have unclear and overlapping business functionality.

RETAIN: Largely self contained, with well defined asset, process and system boundaries. These services are aligned with and are relevant to the organization's strategy

REFACTOR: Often services that meet the technical and functional criteria of the organization display fuzzy process or system boundaries. In these cases, the service can often be refactored to include only the core functionality, with common services used to provide the remainder.

RETIRE: Retire services that do not meet minimum levels of technical and functional fitness.

RATIONALIZE: Used to address portfolios that offer services which in fact are composed of multiple releases of the same operating system, service or application etc.

Service Retirement
An often over looked investment, this is potentially one of the largest hidden costs in a service providers organization, particularly in a large organization with a long history. Few providers have a clear plan for retiring increasingly redundant services. This is often due to a number of reasons, including a lack of visibility of what services are actually offered, and the fear that retiring a service may impact other services being offered.

Refreshing the Portfolio
As conditions and markets change, some services may no longer be required.
- The CIO must monitor, measure, reassess and make changes as business needs change
- By organizing an efficient portfolio with optimal levels of Return on Investment (ROI) and risk, the organization maximizes the value realization on its resources and capabilities.

4.3.3 Demand Management

GOAL: To assist the IT Service Provider in understanding and influencing Customer demand for Services and the provision of Capacity to meet these demands.

Demand Management was previously an activity found within Capacity Management, and now within Version 3 of ITIL® it has been made a separate process found within the Service Strategy phase. The reasoning behind this is that before we decide how to design for capacity, decisions must be made regarding why demand should be managed in a particular way. Such questions asked here include:

- Why does the business need this capacity?
- Does the benefit of providing the required capacity outweigh the costs?
- Why should the demand for services be managed to align with the IT strategic objectives?

Demand Management is responsible for understanding and strategically responding to business demands for services by:

- Analysing patterns of activity and user profiles.
- Provisioning capacity in line with strategic objectives.

Two ways to influence or manage demand:

1. Physical/Technical constraints
   (E.g. restrict number of connections, users, running times)
2. Financial constraints
   (E.g. using expensive charging for services near full capacity or over capacity quotas)

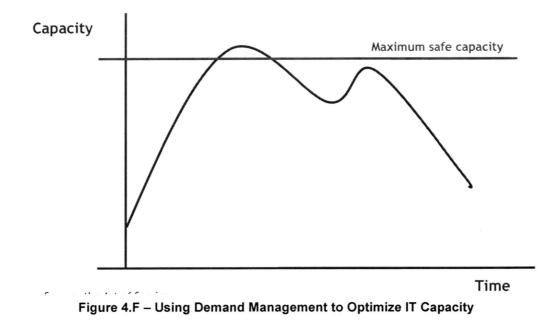

Figure 4.F – Using Demand Management to Optimize IT Capacity

QUESTION:

Every morning between 8:00am and 8:30am, approximately 1500 users logon to the network. At the same time, many IT services, batch jobs and reports are run by various groups throughout the organization.

Recently the performance of the IT infrastructure has been experiencing problems during this time period (e.g. Taking a long time to log on, reports and batch jobs failing) Outside of this time, the IT infrastructure performs at acceptable levels.

What are some Demand Management techniques that could be utilized to address this situation?

Example responses:
- Staggering work start times
- Prioritizing reports and batch jobs
- Running non-time-critical reports and batch jobs at night or outside typical work hours
- Restricting any non-critical activities during peak periods.

Analyzing Patterns of Business Activity (PBA)

Business processes are the primary source of demand for services. Patterns of business activity (PBA) influence the demand patterns seen by the service providers.

It is very important to study the customer's business to identify, analyze and codify such patterns to provide sufficient basis for capacity management.

- Analyzing and tracking the activity patterns of the business process make it possible to predict demand for services in the catalogue that support the process.
- Every additional unit of demand generated by business activity is allocated to a unit of service capacity.
- Activity-Based Demand Management can link the demand patterns to ensure that the customers business plans are synchronized with the service management plans of the service provider.

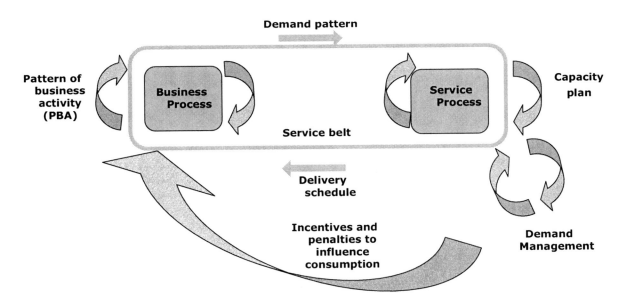

Figure 4.G – Patterns of Business Activity

Keep in mind that Demand Management plays an integral part in supporting the objectives of an organization and maximizing the value of the IT Service Provider. This means that the way in which Demand Management is utilized will vary greatly between each organization. Two examples showing these differences are:

1. **Health Organizations:** When providing IT Services that support critical services being offered to the public, it would be unlikely that any demand management techniques would be utilized, as the impact of these restrictions could lead to tragic implications for patients being treated.

2. **Commercial Confectionery Organizations**: Typically a confectionery company will have extremely busy periods around traditional holidays (E.G Christmas). Demand Management techniques would be utilized to promote more cost-effective use of IT during the non-peak periods, however leading up to these holidays it would be unlikely for any restrictions to be used.

4.4 Service Strategy Summary

The Service Strategy phase enables the organization to ensure that the organizational objectives for IT are defined and that Services and Service Portfolios are maximized for value. Other benefits delivered include:

- Enhanced ability to predict the resources required to fund IT.
- Clearer visibility of the costs for providing IT Services.
- Quality information to support investment decisions in IT.
- Understanding of the use and demand for IT Services, with the ability to influence positive and cost-effective use of IT.

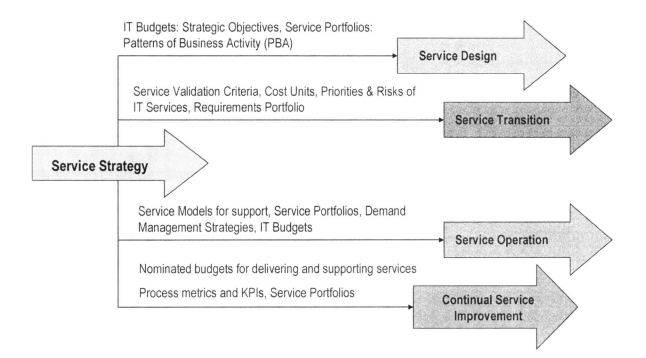

Figure 4.H – Some outputs to other lifecycle phases.

4.5 Service Strategy Service Scenario

To assist with your learning and understanding of how the phases and processes work together, the following scenario will be used throughout this book.

This simplistic overview of a service gives examples of how the processes are utilized to create the service.

> The business has requested that they would like to be able to use the internet for instant messaging with international offices. They are also interested in VOIP and video conferencing. (We shall call this new service HYPE!)

Overall Service Strategy

- It is important here to truly understand exactly what the business needs are, as well as their expectations for this service.
- Value must be defined (utility + warranty = value):
    - Utility – features of HYPE – what type of support will the business require, what features will the business want/need, ie fit for purpose
    - Warranty - levels of service guarantee (continuity, availability, security, capacity) that the business requires needs to be clarified – set out in service level packages:
- Service Level Packages
    - Core service package – instant messaging
    - Supporting service package - added VOIP and/or Video conferencing, ability to attach files
    - Service Level packages – video quality, security of transmissions, access times, service support, user access

Service Portfolio Management

- o You have already been trialing X brand instant messenger service among the IT staff , so it is in your pipeline
- o Can we produce it, or do we need to buy it?
- o Service Catalogue – nil
- o What gap I sit filling in the portfolio?
- o Are there redundant services to retire?

FMIT

- Cost to purchase/build service
- Cost of hardware (web cams, pc upgrades if necessary)
- Cost of increased internet access/bandwidth
- Charging for service????
- Budget?

Demand Management

- When would business most need service? (mornings and afternoons, as they are most likely to interact with international counterparts - time zones), times of year?
- What measures can we take to manage demand?
  - o Limit VOIP/video to certain groups/users
  - o Charge business for use
  - o Dedicated bandwidth across whole of service

By determining the above before you start to design the service, you are in a better position to ensure that HYPE will meet the customer needs (closed loop system). Remember, this is where value is agreed – and Service Operation is where value of HYPE is seen. As we all know, the level of value will more than likely be in direct correlation to the $$ the business is prepared to pay, and this is why it is important to clarify this now, before we start designing.

4.6 Service Strategy Review Questions

These questions also cover the Introduction and Common Terminology Chapters.

Question 1
Which ITIL process is responsible for drawing up a charging system?
  a) Availability Management
  b) Capacity Management
  c) Financial Management for IT Services
  d) Service Level Management

Question 2
What is the RACI model used for?
  a) Documenting the roles and relationships of stakeholders in a process or activity
  b) Defining requirements for a new service or process
  c) Analyzing the business impact of an incident
  d) Creating a balanced scorecard showing the overall status of Service Management

Question 3
Which of the following identifies two Service Portfolio components within the Service Lifecycle?
  a) Requirements Portfolio and Service Catalogue
  b) Service Knowledge Management System and Service Catalogue
  c) Service Knowledge Management System and Requirements Portfolio
  d) Requirements Portfolio and Configuration Management System

Question 4
Which of the following is NOT one of the ITIL core publications?
  a) Service Operation
  b) Service Transition
  c) Service Derivation
  d) Service Strategy

Question 5
A Service Level Package is best described as?
  a) A description of customer requirements used to negotiate a Service Level Agreement
  b) A defined level of utility and warranty associated with a core service package
  c) A description of the value that the customer wants and for which they are willing to pay
  d) A document showing the Service Levels achieved during an agreed reporting period

Question 6
Setting policies and objectives is the primary concern of which of the following elements of the Service Lifecycle?
  a) Service Strategy
  b) Service Strategy and Continual Service Improvement
  c) Service Strategy, Service Transition and Service Operation
  d) Service Strategy, Service Design, Service Transition, Service Operation and Continual Service Improvement

Question 7
A Service owner is responsible for which of the following?
  a) Designing and documenting a Service
  b) Carrying out the Service Operations activities needed to support a Service
  c) Producing a balanced scorecard showing the overall status of all Services
  d) Recommending improvements

Question 8
The utility of a service is best described as:
  a) Fit for design
  b) Fit for purpose
  c) Fit for function
  d) Fit for use

Question 9
The 4 P's of ITSM are people, partners, processes and:
  a) Purpose
  b) Products
  c) Perspectives
  d) Practice

Question 10

The contents of s service package includes:

- a) Base Service Package, Supporting Service Package, Service Level Package
- b) Core Service Package, Supporting Process Package, Service Level Package
- c) Core Service Package, Base Service Package, Service Support Package
- d) Core Service Package, Supporting Services Package, Service Level Packages

5 Service Design_____

Service Design's ultimate concern is the design of new or modified services for introduction into a production (live) environment. It is also concerned with the design of new and modified processes required to deliver and support these services.

Processes:
- Service Level Management (Design)
- Capacity Management
- Availability Management
- IT Service Continuity Management
- Information Security Management
- Supplier Management
- Service Catalogue Management

5.1 Objectives

There are three main objectives of the Service Design lifecycle phase:
- To convert the strategic objectives defined during Service Strategy into Services and Service Portfolios.
- To use a holistic approach for design to ensure integrated end-to-end business related functionality and quality.
- To ensure consistent design standards and conventions are followed.

5.2 Major Concepts

An overall, integrated approach should be adopted for the design activities, covering five major aspects of Service Design

1. **Service Portfolio:** Service Management systems and tools, especially the Service Portfolio for the management and control of services through their lifecycle.
2. **Service Solutions:** including all of the functional requirements, resources and capabilities needed and agreed.
3. **Technology architectures:** Technology architectures and management architectures and tools required to provide the service.
4. **Processes:** Processes needed to design, transition, operate and improve the service.
5. **Measurement systems:** Measurement systems, methods and metrics for the services, the architectures and their constituent components and the processes.

The key aspect in the design of new or changed services is to meet changing business needs. Every time a new service solution is produced, it needs to be checked against each of the other aspects to ensure that it will integrate and interface with all of the other services in existence.

Service Design Packages

The information contained within a Service Design Package including all aspects of the service and its requirements is used to provide guidance and structure through all of the subsequent stages of its lifecycle. A Service Design Package is produced for each new IT Service, major Change, or IT Service Retirement.

Service Design Packages

- Business Requirements
- Service Applicability
- Service Contacts
- Service Functional Requirements
- Service Level Requirements
- Service Design & Topology

- Organizational Readiness Assessment
- User Acceptance Test Criteria
- Service Program
- Service Transition Plan
- Service Operational Plan
- Service Acceptance Criteria

5.3 Service Design Processes

The processes included with the Service Design lifecycle phase are:
- Service Level Management (Design)
- Capacity Management
- Availability Management
- IT Service Continuity Management
- Information Security Management
- Supplier Management
- Service Catalogue Management

It is important to note that many of the activities from these processes will occur in other lifecycle phases, especially Service Operation. Additionally, Service Level Management also plays an important role in Continual Service Improvement.

5.3.1 Service Level Management

GOAL: To ensure that the levels of IT service delivery are achieved, both for existing services and new services in accordance with the agreed targets.

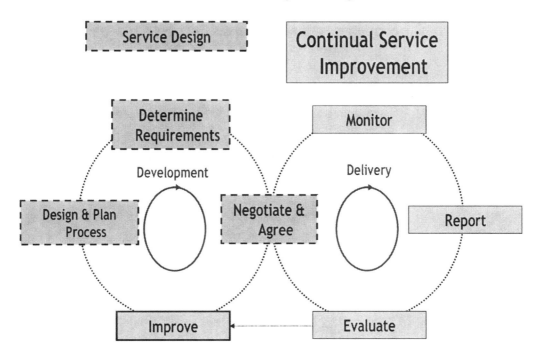

During the Service Design lifecycle phase, Service Level Management:
- Designs and plans the SLM process and Service Level Agreement (SLA) Structure.
- Determines the Service Level Requirements (SLRs)
- Negotiates and Agrees upon the relevant Service Level targets with customers to produce Service Level Agreements

Negotiates and agrees upon the support elements required by the internal IT groups and External Suppliers to produce Operational Level Agreements (internal) and Underpinning Contracts (external).

Terminology	Explanation
Service Level Agreements (SLAs):	Written agreement between a service provider and Customers that document agreed Service Levels for a Service.
Service Catalogue:	Written statement of available IT services, default levels, options, prices and which business processes or customers use them.
Underpinning Contract (UCs):	Contract with an external supplier that supports the IT organization in their delivery of services.
Operational Level Agreement (OLAs)	Internal agreement which supports the IT organization in their delivery of services.
Service Level Requirements	Detailed recording of the Customer's needs, forming the design criteria for a new or modified service.

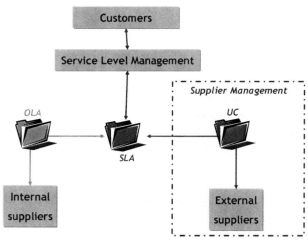

Figure 5.A – SLAs, OLAs and UCs

Negotiating and Agreeing upon the SLAs and OLAs is the responsibility of Service Level Management. Supplier Management is responsible for negotiation and agreeing upon Underpinning Contracts with external suppliers. These two processes must communicate to ensure that the Underpinning Contracts do align with and support the SLAs in place.

What are the roles of OLAs and UCs?
They are agreements with the internal IT departments and external suppliers on how they support the IT organization in meeting the Service Level Agreements with customers.

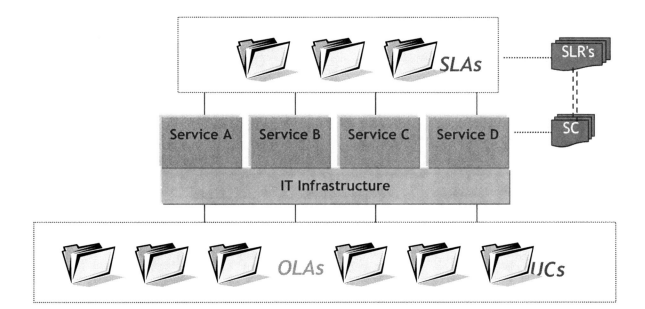

Figure 5.B – How it all fits together

Question?
According to the ITIL® framework which of these documents should be developed first?
The Service Catalogue: because you need to know what we are providing first, and then we can map the customer requirements to the Service Catalogue to see what gaps or redundant service exist.

The Service Catalogue

Figure 5.C below demonstrates the Business Service Catalogue and Technical Service Catalogues and the different views they represent. Service Level Management supports Service Catalogue Management in the creation of a customer facing Business Service Catalogue, ensuring that all current (live) services are represented here.

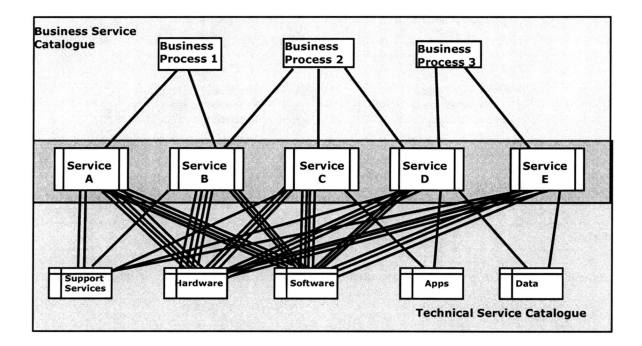

Figure 5.C – The Service Catalogue

Service Level Agreement Structures

There are a number of ways in which Service Level Agreements can be structured. The important factors to consider when choosing the SLA structure are:

- Will the SLA allow flexibility in the levels of service to be delivered for various customers?
- Will the SLA structure require a lot of duplication of effort?
- Who will sign the SLAs?

Three types of SLAs structures that are discussed within ITIL® are Service-based, Customer-based and Multi-level or Hierarchical SLAs.

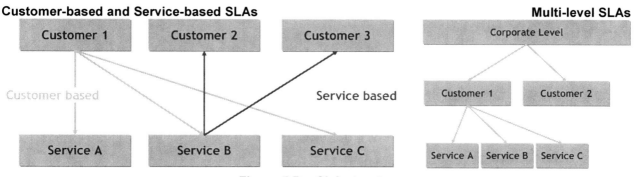

Figure 5.D – SLA structures

Many different factors will need to be considered when deciding which SLA structure is most appropriate for an organization to use.

Typical Multi-level SLA Structure components:
1. **Corporate level:** All generic issues are covered, which are the same for the entire organization.
Example: *The Corporate Security Baseline, e.g. Passwords, ID cards etc.*
2. **Customer level:** Those issues specific to a customer can be dealt with.
Example: *Security requirements of one or more departments within the organization are higher: E.g. The financial department needs higher security measures.*
3. **Service Level:** All issues relevant to a specific service (in relation to customer) can be covered.
Example: *The email services for a particular department needs encryption and secure backups.*

Using a multi-level structure for a large organization reduces the duplication of effort while still providing customization for customers and services (inheritance).

The Contents of Service Level Agreements:
- Introduction
- Service hours
- Availability targets
- Reliability
- Support arrangements
- Transaction response times
- Disaster Recovery
- Reporting requirements
- Incentives and Penalties

See the Continual Service Improvement Chapter for the aspects of Service Level Management that focus on improving the level of quality being delivered for IT Services.

5.3.2 Capacity Management

GOAL: To ensure the current and future capacity and performance demands of the customer regarding IT service provision are delivered against justifiable costs.

Capacity Management is the process that manages:
- the right capacity,
- at the right location,
- at the right moment,
- for the right customer,
- against the right costs

Capacity Management provides the predictive and ongoing capacity indicators needed to align capacity to demand. It is about finding the right balance between resources and capabilities, and demand.

- Too many resources & capabilities = ↑ $$$$

- Too little resources & capabilities = ↓ performance

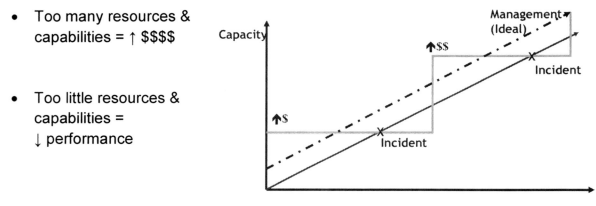

Figure 5.E - The Consequences of Reactive Behaviour

This graph represents the consequences of reactive behaviour in managing capacity.
- Diagonal solid line represents the typical capacity needs of an organization over time.
- The dotted line represents the Ideal management of capacity to meet the organization's needs.
- The Horizontal lines depicts the reactive approach, whereby $$ are put into resolving capacity issues, only when it becomes an issue. This goes well until the next major incident, and more reactive $$ are injected to try and "fix" the capacity issues, rather than addressing the issue in a proactive manner.

Sub-Processes of Capacity Management:

Business Capacity Management:
- Manage Capacity to meet future business requirements for IT services
- Plan and implement sufficient capacity in an appropriate timescale
- Should be included in Change Management and Project management activities

Service Capacity Management
- Focus on managing ongoing service performance as detailed in SLA or SLR
- Establish baselines and profiles of use of Services

Component Capacity Management
Identify and manage each of the components of the IT Infrastructure
- E.g. CPU, memory, disks, network bandwidth
- Evaluates NEW technology
- Load balances across resources

All 3 components collate their data and report to Service Level Management and Financial Management for IT Services.

Activities

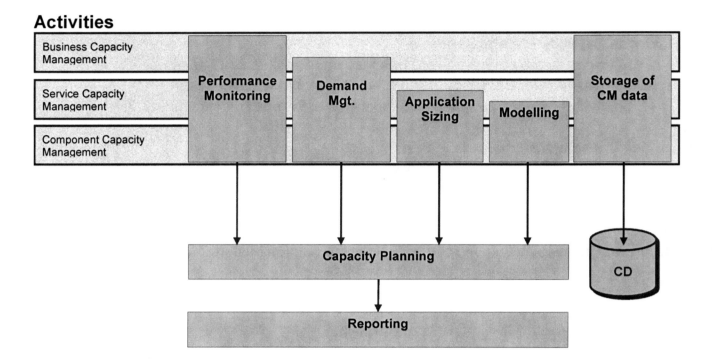

Figure 5.F – Activities of Capacity Management

Capacity Management has 6 main activities:

1. **Performance Monitoring -** Measuring, monitoring, and tuning the performance of *IT Infrastructure components.*
2. **Demand Management -** Short term reactive implementation of strategies considered in Service Strategy to manage current demand
3. **Application Sizing -** Determining the hardware or network capacity to support new or modified applications and the predicted workload.
4. **Modelling -** Used to forecast the behaviour of the infrastructure *under certain conditions.*
5. Storage of Capacity Management Data
6. Capacity Planning
7. Reporting

Roles and Responsibilities for Capacity Management:

Capacity Manager:
<u>Role</u>
To ensure adequate performance and capacity for all IT services.

<u>Responsibilities:</u>
Capacity Plan (development and management)
Oversee Performance and Capacity monitoring & alerting
Report provision and advice

<u>Skills:</u>
Strategic business awareness, technical, analytical, consultancy

Capacity Management is critical for ensuring effective and efficient capacity and performance IT Services and IT components in line with business requirements and overall IT strategic objectives. It is essential that the Capacity Manager ensures that the process utilizes information from and provides information to all phases of the Service Lifecycle.

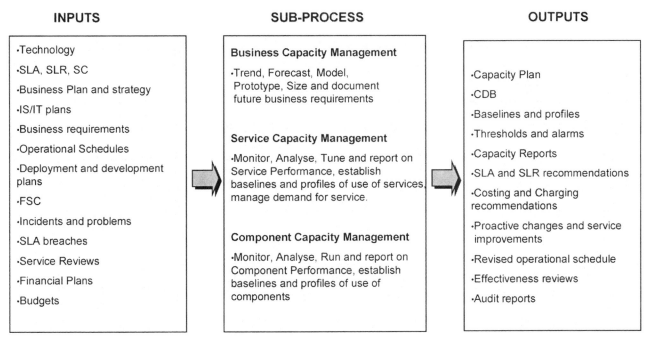

Figure 5.G – Capacity Management relationships with the rest of ITIL®

5.3.3 Availability Management

GOAL: To optimize the capability of the IT infrastructure and supporting the organization to deliver a cost effective and sustained level of availability that enables the business to satisfy its objectives.

Other Availability objectives are:
- Reduction in the frequency and duration of Availability related incidents.
- Maintain a forward looking Availability plan.

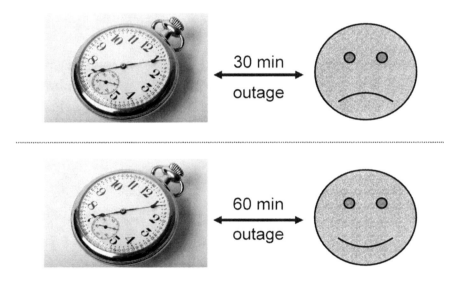

Figure 5.H – The Perception of Availability

Question?

Why could users be happy with a 60 minute outage and unhappy with 30 minute outage?

A1: 30min outage during peak time, overtime being paid to staff, urgent report required.
A2: 60min outage on weekend, holiday, off peak, when service not required.
A3: 30min outage on critical IT Service, 60min outage on non-critical IT Service.
A4: 30mins unplanned outage, 60min planned outage (e.g. maintenance).

For a consumer/user of an IT Service, its Availability and Reliability can directly influence both the perception and satisfaction of the overall IT Service provision.

Proactive and Reactive Elements of Availability Management:

Proactive activities:
Involves the proactive planning, design and improvement of availability. These activities are principally involved within design and planning roles.
(Service Design Phase)

Reactive activities:
Involves the monitoring, measuring, analysis and management of all events, incidents and problems regarding availability.

(Service Operation Phase)

Terminology	Explanation
Availability:	The ability of an IT Service or component to perform its *required function* at a stated instant or over a *stated period* of time.
Security:	Information Security Management *determines requirements*, Availability Management *implements measures*
Reliability:	*Freedom* from operational failure.
Resilience:	The ability to **withstand failure.**
Maintainability: (internal)	The ability of an IT component to be retained in or restored to, an operational state. Based on skills, knowledge, technology, backups, availability of IT staff.
Serviceability: (external)	The contractual obligation / arrangements made with 3rd party external suppliers. Measured by Availability, Reliability and Maintainability of IT Service and components under control of the external suppliers. Managed by Supplier Management through Underpinning Contracts.
Vital Business Function (VBF):	The **business critical elements** of the business process supported by an IT Service.

Activities

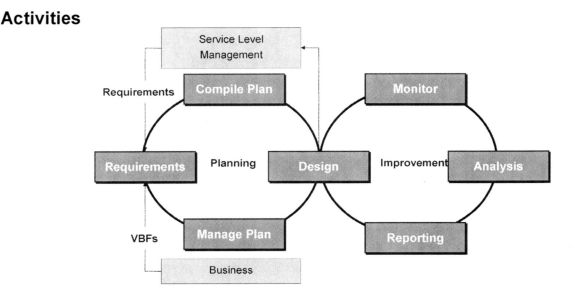

Figure 5.I – Availability Activities

Activities involved in Availability Management can form two continuous cycles of Planning and Improvement.

Availability Management and Incident Management:

An aim of Availability Management is to ensure the duration and impact from Incidents impacting IT Services are minimised, to enable business operations to resume as quickly as possible.

The expanded Incident lifecycle enables the total IT Service downtime for any given Incident to be broken down and mapped against the major stages that all Incidents go through.

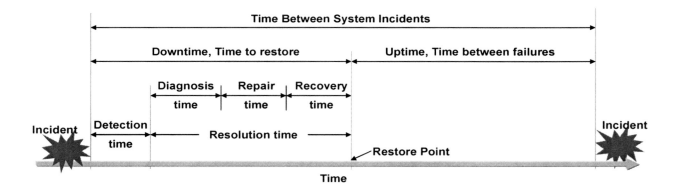

Figure 5.J – The Expanded Incident Lifecycle

Lifecycle of an Incident. (Availability Management Metrics)

Mean time between Failures (MTBF) or *uptime*
- Average time between the recovery from one incident and the occurrence of the next incident, relates to the reliability of the service

Mean time to Restore Service (MTRS) or *downtime*
- Average time taken to restore a CI or IT service after a failure.
- Measured from when CI or IT service fails until it is fully restored and delivering its normal functionality.

Mean time between System Incidents (MTBSI):
- Average time between the occurrence of two consecutive incidents.
- Sum of the MTRS and MTBF.

Relationships:
- high ratio of MTBF/MTBSI indicates there are many minor faults
- low ratio of MTBF/MTBSI indicates there are few major faults

Detection Time: Time for the service provider to be **informed** of the fault. **(reported)**

Diagnosis Time: Time for the service provider to respond after **diagnosis** completed

Repair Time:
Time the service provider restores the components that caused the fault.
Calculated from **diagnosis** to **recovery** time

Restoration Time: (MTRS)
The **agreed** level of service is restored to the user.
Calculated from **detection** to **restore point.**

Restore Point:
The point where the agreed level of service has been restored

Roles and Responsibilities

Availability Manager:
Role:
To ensure adequate availability of all IT services.

Responsibilities:
Availability Plan (development and management)
Availability monitoring & alerting
Report provision and advice

Skills:
Awareness of how IT supports the business,
Technical, analytical, consultancy,
Seeks continuous improvement

NOTE: The Availability Manager does not seek to achieve 100% Availability, but instead seeks to deliver Availability that matches or exceeds (within reason) the business requirements.

5.3.4 IT Service Continuity Management

GOAL: To support the overall Business Continuity Management by ensuring that the required IT infrastructure and the IT service provision can be recovered within required and agreed business time scales. ** Often referred to as Disaster Recovery planning. **

Terminology	Explanation
Disaster:	NOT part of **daily operational activities** and requires a **separate system**. (Not necessarily a flood, fire etc. may be due to a blackout or power problem and the SLAs are in danger of being breached).
Business Continuity Management: (BCM)	Strategies and actions to take place to continue Business Processes in the case of a disaster. It is essential that the ITSCM strategy is integrated into and a subset of the BCM strategy.
Business Impact Analysis: (BIA)	Quantifies the impact loss of IT service would have on the business.
Risk Assessment:	Evaluate *Assets*, *threats* and *vulnerabilities*.
Scope:	The scope of IT Service Continuity Management considers all identified critical business processes and IT service(s) that underpin them. This may include hardware, software, essential services and utilities, critical paper records, courier services, voice services & physical location areas e.g. offices, data centres etc.

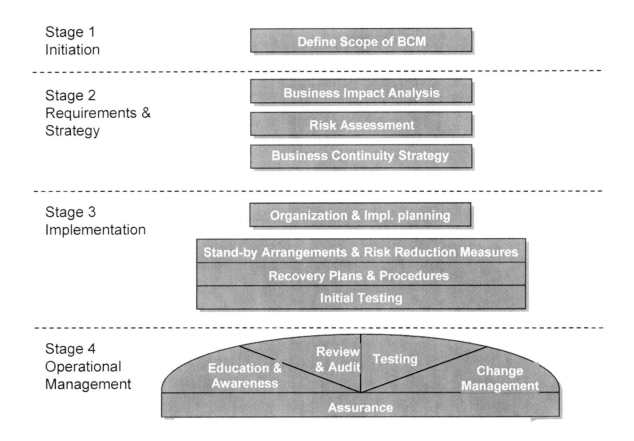

Figure 5.K – Activities of IT Service Continuity Management

Key Activities of IT Service Continuity Management:

Performing a Business Impact Analysis (BIA) identifies:
- Critical business processes & Vital Business Functions
- Potential damage or loss caused by disruption
- Possible escalations caused by damage or loss
- Necessary resources required to enable continuity of critical business processes
- Time constraints for minimum recovery of facilities and services
- Time constraints for complete recovery of facilities and services

Risk Assessment:
- Gather information on assets (IT infrastructure components),
- Threats from both Internal & external sources (the likelihood of occurring)
- Vulnerabilities (the extent of impact or effect on organization)

Developing Countermeasures (Recovery and Risk Reduction Measures):

Terminology	Explanation
Counter Measures:	Measures to prevent or *recover* from disaster
Manual Workaround:	Using *non-IT* based solution to overcome IT service disruption
Gradual recovery:	Aka *Cold* standby (>72hrs to recover from a 'Disaster').
Intermediate Recovery:	Aka *Warm* standby (24-72hrs to recover from a 'Disaster')
Immediate Recovery:	Aka *Hot* standby (< 24hrs, usually implies 1-2 hrs to recover from a 'Disaster)
Reciprocal Arrangement:	Agreement with another similar sized company to share disaster recovery obligations

Operational Management:
- Education & awareness
- Training
- Reviews
- Ongoing testing
  - At least annually
  - Following major changes
- Audits of recovery procedures, risk-reduction measures and for compliance to procedures.

Roles and Responsibilities:

Role	Responsibilities and Skills
Board	Crisis Management Corporate/Business decisions External affairs
Senior Management	Co-ordination Direction and arbitration Resource authorization
Management	Invocation of continuity or recovery Team Leadership Site Management Liaison & Reporting
Supervisors and Staff	Task execution Team membership Team and Site liaison

Typical responsibilities for ITSCM in planning and dealing with disaster are similar to how First Aid Officers and Fire Wardens act in planning and operational roles.

Skill requirements for ITSCM Manager and staff:
- Knowledge of the business (help set priorities)
- Calm under pressure
- Analytical (problem solving)
- Leadership and Team players
- Negotiation and Communication

5.3.5 Information Security Management

GOAL*:* To align IT security with business security and ensure that information security is effectively managed in all service and IT Service Management activities.

Information Security Management ensures that the **confidentiality**, **integrity** and **availability** of an organization's assets, information, data and IT services is maintained. Information Security Management must consider the following four perspectives:

- Organizational
- Procedural
- Physical
- Technical

Terminology	Explanation
Confidentiality:	Protecting information against unauthorized access and use. Examples: *Passwords, swipe cards, firewalls*
Integrity:	Accuracy, completeness and timeliness of the information. Examples: *Rollback mechanisms, test procedures, audits.*
Availability:	The information should be accessible at any agreed time. This depends on the continuity provided by the information processing systems. Examples: *UPS, resilient systems, Service desk hours*
Security Baseline:	The security level adopted by the IT organization for its own security and from the point of view of good 'due diligence'. Possible to have multiple baselines Examples: *Security access based employee rank/title*
Security Incident:	Any incident that may interfere with achieving the SLA security requirements; materialisation of a threat Examples: *Security Breach or potential weakness*

Figure 5.L – Factors influencing Information Security Management

Information Security Management (ISM) needs to be considered within the overall corporate governance framework. This provides the *strategic* direction for security activities and ensures objectives are achieved. It further ensures that the information security risks are appropriately managed and that the enterprise information resources are used responsibly.

The purpose of ISM is to provide a focus for all aspects of IT security and manage all IT activities.

Activities

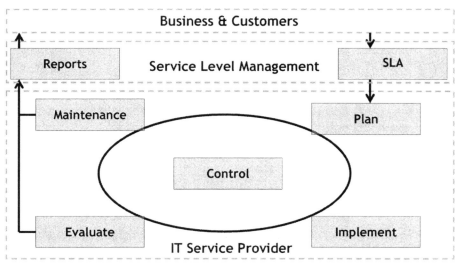

Figure 5.M – Activities of Information Security Management

Control:

The activity of Control has a central place in the above figure, as this is where Information Security is actually enforced in an organization. The way in which this is done is shown below.

Prevention
Reduction

Detection/
Repression

Correction/
Recovery

Evaluation

Threat

Incident

Damage

Control

There are various security threats to our infrastructure and we want to prevent or reduce the damage of these as much as possible.

In the case that they do pass our prevention mechanisms, we need to have detection techniques to identify when and where they occurred.

Once a security incident has occurred, we want to repress or minimize the damage associated with this incident.
We then want to correct any damage caused and recover our infrastructure to normal levels.

After this process we need to review how and why the breach occurred and how successful were we in responding to the breach.

Roles and Responsibilities

Information Security Manager
Responsibilities:
- Manage entire security process,
- Consult with senior management

Skills:
- Strategic Sense of PR, tactical.

Security Officer
Responsibilities:
- Day to day operational duties,
- Advise staff on security policy & measures

Skills:
- Analytical, eye for detail, consultancy

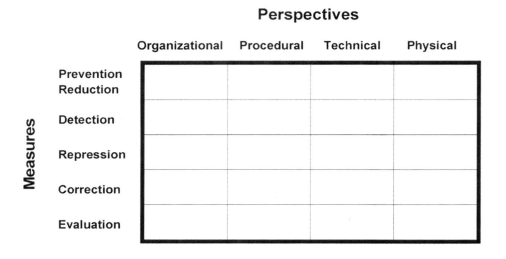

Figure 5.N – Activities of Information Security Management

The Information Security Measure Matrix is a useful tool in performing a gap analysis:
- Ensures there is a balance in measures
- Avoids a concentration of measures in either a certain perspective (eg technical) or of a certain measure (eg detection).

Remember: ultimately it's a **cost-benefit analysis** that determines how much you invest in security.

5.3.6 Supplier Management

GOAL: To manage suppliers and the services they supply, to provide seamless quality of IT service to the business and ensure that value for money is obtained.

Terminology	Explanation
Supplier service improvement plans: (SSIP)	Used to record all improvement actions and plans agreed between suppliers and service providers.
Supplier Survey Reports:	Feedback gathered from all individuals that deal directly with suppliers throughout their day to day role. Results are collated and reviewed by Supplier Management, to ensure consistency in quality of service provided by suppliers in all areas.
Supplier & Contract performance reports:	Used as input for the Supplier & Contract review meetings to manage the quality of the service provided by suppliers and partners. This should include information on shared risk, when appropriate.
Types of Supplier Arrangements:	
Co-sourcing:	An informal combination of insourcing and outsourcing, using a number of outsourcing organizations working together to co-source key elements within the lifecycle.
Partnership or multi-sourcing:	Formal arrangements between two or more organizations to work together to design, develop transition, maintain, operate, and/or support IT service(s). The focus here tends to be on strategic partnerships that leverage critical expertise or market opportunities.
Business Process Outsourcing:	Formal arrangements where an external organization provides and manages the other organization's entire business process(es) or functions(s) in a low cost location. Common examples are accounting, payroll and call centre operations.

Knowledge Process Outsourcing: This is a **new enhancement** of Business Process Outsourcing, where external organizations provide domain based processes and business expertise rather than just process expertise and requires advanced analytical and specialized skills from the outsourcing organization.

Application Service Provision: Where external organizations provide shared computer based services to customer organizations over a network. The complexities and costs of such shared software can be reduced and provided to organizations that could otherwise not justify the investment.

Supplier and Contact Database (SCD):

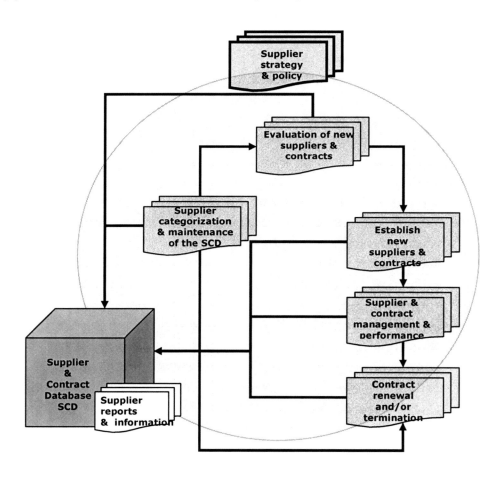

Figure 5.O – The Supplier & Contract Database

All Supplier Management process activity should be driven by supplier strategy and policy. In order to achieve consistency and effectiveness in the implementation of the policy, a Supplier and Contract Database (SCD) should be established.

Ideally the SCD should form an integrated element of a comprehensive CMS(Configuration Management System) or SKMS(Service Knowledge Management System), recording all supplier and contract details, together with the types of service, products etc provided by each supplier, and all the other information and relationships with other associated CIs(Configuration Items).
This will also so contribute to the information held in the Service Portfolio and Catalogue.

Relationships with other Lifecycle Phases:

The information within the SCD will provide a complete set of reference information for all Supplier Management procedures and activities needed across the Service Lifecycle. Such activities include:

Lifecycle Phase	Activities
Service Design	• Supplier categorization and maintenance of the SCD • Evaluation and set-up of new suppliers and contracts
Service Design	• Assessing the transition to new suppliers • Establishing new suppliers
Service Operation	• Supplier and Contract Management and performance • Contract renewal and termination
Continual Service Improvement	• Identifying improvement actions involving suppliers. • Collating measurements gather on supplier arrangements.

This table shows that although Supplier Management is firmly placed within the Service Design Phase of the Lifecycle, many activities are carried out in the other Lifecycle Phases too.

5.3.7 Service Catalogue Management

GOAL: To ensure that a Service Catalogue is produced, maintained and contains accurate information on all operational services and those ready for deployment.

The Service Catalogue has two aspects:

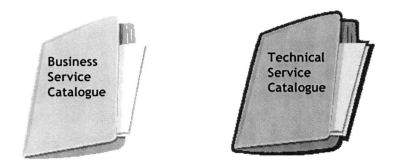

Business Service Catalogue: contains details of all the IT service delivered to the customer, together with relationships to the business units and the business process that rely on the IT services. This is the customer view of the Service Catalogue.

Technical Service Catalogue: contains details of all the IT service delivered to the customer, together with relationships to the supporting services, shared services, components and Configuration Items necessary to support the provision of the service to the business. This should underpin the Business Service Catalogue and *not form part of the customer view.*

5.4 Service Design Summary

Good Service Design means it is possible to deliver quality, cost effective services and to ensure that the business requirements are being met. It also delivers:
- Improved Quality of Service
- Improved Consistency of Service
- Improved Service Alignments
- Standards and Conventions to be followed
- More Effective Service Performance

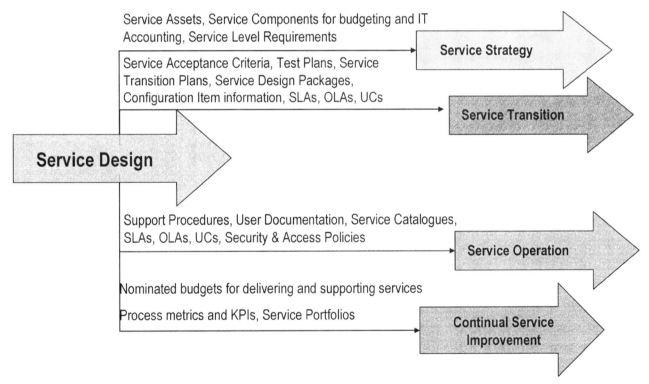

Figure 5.M – Some outputs to other lifecycle phases.

5.5 Service Design Scenario

Service Level Management
- SLR – detailed requirements that constitute the design criteria to be met. Eg secure, clear uninterrupted voice, real time video etc
- SLA structure – decided to go with multi level (based on decision of service level package used, as well as offering greater security and accessibility to various departments/users.)

Capacity Management
- **Application Sizing** – assessing what minimum pc requirements needed to support new HYPE software, as well as type of webcam to best provide service, network bandwwidth
- **Modelling** – how many users can videoconference before quality of service is affected – throughput/bandwidth targets? How may this service impact on other services?
- **Demand Management** – designing to ensure ability to limit bandwidth/video access during peak times for certain users/groups

Availability Management
- To ensure availability targets are met, regular maintenance of components required, as well as ensuring through Supplier mgt that ISP UC is met (serviceability requirements).
- If business wants 24/7 access, then design of redundant systems may be required… at a cost!

Information Security Management
- Confidentiality – user passwords design (eg HYPE service is not controlled locally – all information is stored on vendor's servers. If all users use same password as network login, resulting in a clear pattern, then it would be possible for security to be threatened if "someone" hacked into vendor server)
- Integrity – will logs of all conversations/messages/video kept ad stored?
- Availability – having those logs available to those who require it, when they require it

Service Catalogue Management

- Business Service Catalogue – will describe HYPE service as business understands it, including levels of service
- Technical Services Catalogue – will clearly list technical and supporting service information, eg ISP bandwidth, server requirements etc...

ITSCM

- The business has decided that this is a BCP, so standby arrangements are negotiated with business ($$)
- Decided that the telephone line and/or email will be possible recovery measures until service is restored – included in ITSCM plan

Supplier Management

Negotiate UCs with software vendor, ISP, WAN
Monitor external supplier service – discussions with Availability Mgt, Service Desk etc

The Service Design processes will ensure that HYPE meets the customer needs and can continue to be supported during the Service Operation phase.

5.6 Service Design Review Questions

Question 1
Which ITIL process analyses threats and dependencies to IT Services as part of the decision regarding "countermeasures" to be implemented?
a) Availability Management
b) IT Service Continuity Management
c) Problem Management
d) Service Asset & Configuration Management

Question 2
What is the name of the activity within the Capacity Management process whose purpose is to predict the future capacity requirements of new and changed services?
a) Application Sizing
b) Demand Management
c) Modeling
d) Tuning

Question 3
In which ITIL process are negotiations held with the customer about the availability and capacity levels to be provided?
a) Availability Management
b) Capacity Management
c) Financial Management for IT Services
d) Service Level Management

Question 4
Which of the following BEST describes a Virtual Service Desk structure?
a) A Service Desk that also provides onsite technical support to its users
b) A Service Desk where analysts only speak one language
c) A Service Desk that is situated in the same location as the users it serves
d) A Service Desk that could be in any physical location but uses telecommunications and systems to make it appear that they are in the same location

Question 5
Which of the following activities is Service Level Management responsible for?
a) Informing users of available services
b) Identifying customer needs
c) Overseeing service release schedule
d) Keeping accurate records of all configuration items

Question 6
Which process reviews Operational Level Agreements (OLAs) on a regular basis?
a) Supplier Management
b) Service Level Management
c) Service Portfolio Management
d) Contract Management

Question 7
What is another term for Uptime?
a) Mean Time Between Failures (MTBF)
b) Mean Time to Restore Service (MTRS)
c) Mean Time Between System Incidents (MTBSI)
d) Relationship between MTBF and MTBSI

Question 8
Which of the following is an activity of IT Service Continuity Management?
a) advising end users of a system failure
b) documenting the fallback arrangements
c) reporting regarding availability
d) guaranteeing that the Configuration Items are constantly kept up-to-date.

Question 9
Information security must consider the following four perspectives:
 I. Organizational
 II. Physical
 III. Technical
 IV. ?

 a) Process
 b) Security
 c) Procedural
 d) Firewalls

Question 10
The 3 types of Service Level Agreements are:
 a) Customer based, Service based, Corporate based
 b) Corporate level, customer level, service level
 c) Service based, customer based, user based
 d) Customer based, service base, multi-level based

6 Service Transition

The Service Transition lifecycle phase focuses on the vulnerable transition between the Design phase and the Operation phase of a service. It is particularly critical as functional and technical errors not found during this phase will result in significantly higher impact levels to the business and/or IT infrastructure and will usually cost much more to fix once the Service is in operation.

Processes:
- Knowledge Management
- Service Asset & Configuration Management
- Change Management
- Release & Deployment Management
- Validation and Testing

6.1 Objectives

The development and improvement of capabilities for transitioning new and changed services into operation.

Other objectives include:
- To ensure that new and changed services meet customer requirements and do not adversely impact the IT infrastructure or business processes.
- To reduce the variation between estimated and actual costs, timeframes, risks and impact scales.

6.2 Major Concepts

Components, Tools and Databases

The execution of any IT Service Management process usually requires access to, or storage of, relevant sets of data and information. As the Service Transition phase incorporates the processes of Knowledge Management and Service Asset & Configuration Management, which are heavily focussed on the management of data, information and knowledge, the components, tools and databases needed to do this are discussed during this chapter.

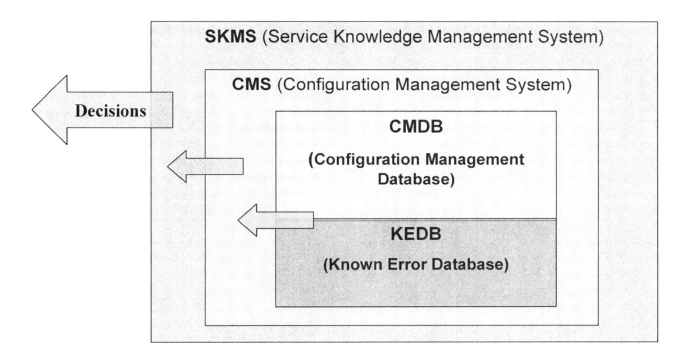

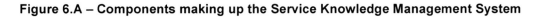

Figure 6.A – Components making up the Service Knowledge Management System

SKMS: Service Knowledge Management System (SKMS):
The complete set of tools and databases that are used to manage knowledge and information. The SKMS includes the Configuration Management System as well as other tools and databases. The SKMS stores, manages, updates and presents all information that an IT service provider needs to manage the full lifecycle of its services. The main purpose of the

SKMS is to provide quality information so that informed decisions can be made by the IT service provider.

CMS: Configuration Management System:

A set of tools and databases that are used to manage an IT service provider's configuration data. The CMS also includes information about incidents, problems, known errors, changes and releases; and may contain data about employees, suppliers' locations, business units, customers and users. The CMS is maintained by Service Asset & Configuration Management and is used by all IT Service Management processes. Two major components are the:

- **CMDB: Configuration Management Database**

- **KEDB: Known Error Database.** This database is created by Problem Management and used by Incident and Problem Management.

6.3 Service Transition Processes

6.3.1 Knowledge Management

GOAL: To enable organizations to improve the quality of management decision making by ensuring that reliable and secure information and data is available throughout the service lifecycle.

The primary purpose is to improve efficiency by reducing the need to rediscover knowledge. This requires accessible, quality and relevant data and information to be available to staff.

Benefits that a successful Knowledge Management System would deliver to the business and IT organization:
*   We can stop having to continually reinvent the wheel
*   More efficient use of resources (including people)
*   Enables the organization to continually mature and develop.

Challenges you would see in implementing and operating a Knowledge Management System:
*   Getting staff to use the systems.
*   Having the extra time required to record relevant information and knowledge after actions are made.
*   Managing information and knowledge that is no longer correct or relevant for the organization.
*   Designing a system that can scale well as an organization grows.

One of the more difficult components of Knowledge Management is ensuring that we do more than simply capture discrete facts about various elements of the organization and IT infrastructure. What this requires is an understanding of the different components and processes required to develop and mature knowledge and wisdom.

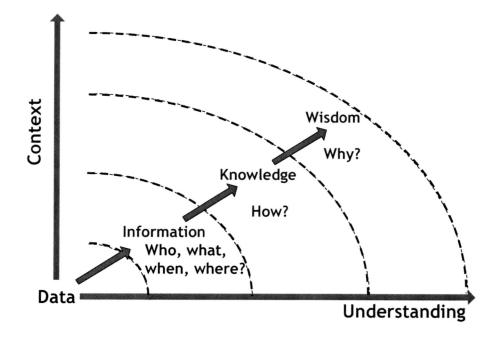

Figure 6.B – Moving from data to wisdom

Data:

Data is a set of discrete facts. Most organizations capture significant amounts of data every day.

Information:

Information comes from providing context to data. This usually requires capturing various sources of data and applying some meaning or relevance to the set of facts.

Knowledge:

Knowledge is composed of the experiences, ideas, insights and judgments from individuals. This usually requires the analysis of information, and is applied in such a way to facilitate decision making.

Wisdom:

Gives the ultimate discernment of the material and having the application and contextual awareness to provide a strong common sense judgment. The use of wisdom ultimately enables an organization to direct its strategy and growth in competitive market spaces.

We can use tools and databases to capture Data, Information and Knowledge, but Wisdom cannot be captured this way, as Wisdom is a concept relating to abilities to use knowledge to make correct judgments and decisions.

6.3.2 Service Asset and Configuration Management

GOAL: To support the agreed IT service provision by managing, storing and providing information about Configuration Items (CI's) and Service Assets throughout their life cycle.

This process manages the service assets and Configuration Items in order to support the other Service Management processes.

Terminology	Explanations
Configuration Item (CI):	*ANY* component that supports an IT service (except people). *Example: IT components or associated items such as Request for Changes, Incident Records, Service Level Agreements.*
Attribute:	*Specific* information about CI's. *Example: Size of RAM, hard drive, bandwidth*
CI Level:	Recording and reporting of CI's at the level that the *business requires* without being overly complex. It's a trade-off balancing the value that the information will provide versus the effort and cost to manage the information over time.
Status Accounting:	Reporting of all *current and historical* data about each CI throughout its lifecycle. *Example: Status = Under Development, being tested, live, withdrawn etc*
Configuration Baseline:	Configuration established at a specific point in time. Captures both the structure and details of a configuration. Used as a reference point for later comparison (e.g. After major changes, disaster recovery etc)

The Configuration Management Database (CDMB):
The CMDB is a set of one or more connected databases and information sources that provide a logical model of the IT infrastructure. It captures Configuration Items (CIs) and the relationships that exist between them. Figure 6.B demonstrates the elements of a CMDB.

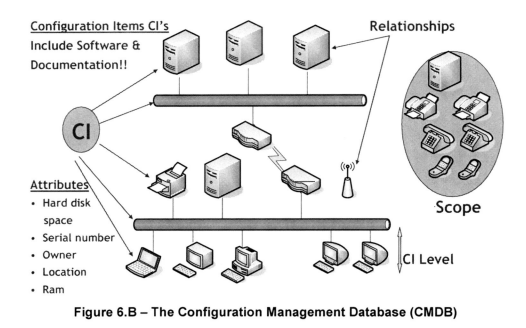

Figure 6.B – The Configuration Management Database (CMDB)

As shown, it is important to determine what level to which the CMDB will record information about the IT infrastructure and to decide what is not covered within the scope of the CMDB. Components out of scope are those typically not under the control of Change Management (e.g. telecommunication equipment)

Activities

Figure 6.C – Configuration Management Activities

Notice how MANAGEMENT & PLANNING are the central activities. Good, sound Service Asset & Configuration Management requires thorough planning for the operation of the process to work.

Planning:
- Defining the strategy, policy, scope, objectives, processes and procedures.
- Roles and responsibilities of involved staff and stakeholders.
- Location of storage areas and libraries used to hold hardware, software and documentation.
- CMDB Design.
- CI naming conventions.
- Housekeeping including license management and archiving of CI's.

Identification:
The selection, identification, labelling and registration of CIs. It is the activity that determine what CIs will be recorded, what their attributes are, and what relationships exist with other CIs. Identification can take place for:
- Hardware and Software – include OS
- Business systems – custom built
- Packages – off the shelf
- Physical databases
- Feeds between databases and links
- Configuration baselines
- Software releases
- Documentation

Control:
Ensures that only authorized and identifiable CIs are recorded from receipt to disposal in order to protect the integrity of the CMDB. Control occurs anytime the CMDB is altered, including:
- Registration of all new CIs and versions
- Update of CI records and licence control
- Updates in connection with RFCs and Change Management
- Update the CMDB after periodic checking of physical items

Status Accounting:
The reporting of all current and historical data concerned with each CI throughout its lifecycle. Provides information on:
- Configuration baselines
- Latest software item versions
- The person responsible for status change
- CI change/incident/problem history

Verification and Audit:
Reviews and audits verify the existence of CIs, checking that they are correctly recorded in the CMDB and that there is conformity between the documented baselines and the actual environment to which they refer.

Configuration Audits should occur at the following times:
- Before and after major changes to the IT infrastructure
- Following recovery from disaster
- In response to the detection of an unauthorized CI
- At regular intervals

The benefits of the CMDB (not necessarily one physical database):
- One tool and not several tools -> reduce costs
- Consistent and visible information about the IT infrastructure available to all staff.
- One team and not several support teams -> reduce costs, improve consistency in CI management
- On stop shop for Configuration queries
- The data about CIs and methods of controlling CIs is consolidated -> reduces auditing effort.
- Opens opportunities for consolidation in CIs to support services.

Roles and Responsibilities

Service Asset Management:
The management of service assets across the whole lifecycle including:
- Full lifecycle management of IT and service assets from acquisitions to disposal
- Maintenance of the asset inventory.

Configuration Management:
- To provide a logical model of the services, assets and infrastructure by recording the relationships between service assets and configuration items.
- To ensure control procedures are complied with to protect the integrity of Configurations.
- To support the information needs of other ITIL® processes.

The actual roles related to Service Asset and Configuration Management includes:
- Service Asset Manager
- Configuration Manager
- Configuration Analyst
- Configuration Administrator/Librarian
- CMS/Tools Administrator
- Change Manager (all Changes to CIs must be authorized by Change Management)

6.3.3 Change Management

GOAL: To ensure that **standardized methods and procedures** are used for controlled, efficient and prompt handling of all Changes, in order to **minimize the impact** of Change-related Incidents upon service quality, and consequently to improve the day-to-day operations of the organization.

"Remember: Not every change is an improvement, but every improvement is a change!"

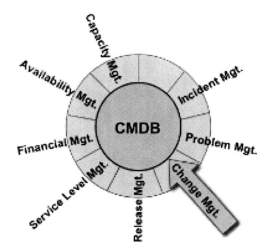

Change Management acts as the greatest contributor to the CMDB, as Changes to CMDB must be assessed and authorized by Change Management first.

To work effectively, Change Management needs to remain impartial to the needs of any one particular IT group or customer, in order to make effective decisions that best support the overall organizational objectives.

Terminology	Explanations
Change:	ANY alteration in the state of a Configuration Item. This includes the addition, modification or removal of approved, supported or baselined hardware, network, software, application, environment, system, desktop build or associated documentation.
Change Models:	Defines how various categories of changes are assessed & authorized, with different mechanisms and activities used to process and deliver changes based on the change type.

NORMAL Change:	A change that follows all of the steps of the change process. It is assessed by either a Change Manager or Change Advisory Board.
STANDARD Change:	A *pre-approved* Change that is low risk, relatively common and follows a procedure or work instruction. E.g. password reset or provision of standard equipment to a new employee. RFCs are not required to implement a Standard Change, and they are logged and tracked using a different mechanism, such as a ***service request.***
EMERGENCY Change:	A change that must be introduced as soon as possible. E.g. to resolve a major incident or implement a security patch. The change management process will normally have a specific procedure for handling Emergency Changes.
Request for Change: **(RFC)**	Standard form to capture and process ALL Changes to any CI
Forward Schedule of Changes (FSC):	Schedule of Approved Changes and proposed implementation dates. The Service Desk should communicate this to the users.
Projected Service Outage (PSO):	Details of Changes to agreed SLAs and service availability because of the Forward Schedule of Change in addition to planned downtime from other causes such as planned maintenance and data backups.
Change Advisory Board: **(CAB)**	A group that provides expert advice to the Change Manager. Involves representatives from various IT and business areas as well as other involved stakeholders including external suppliers. Chaired by the Change Manager
Emergency CAB: **(ECAB)**	Subgroup of CAB to provide expert advice on urgent Change matters.

Activities:

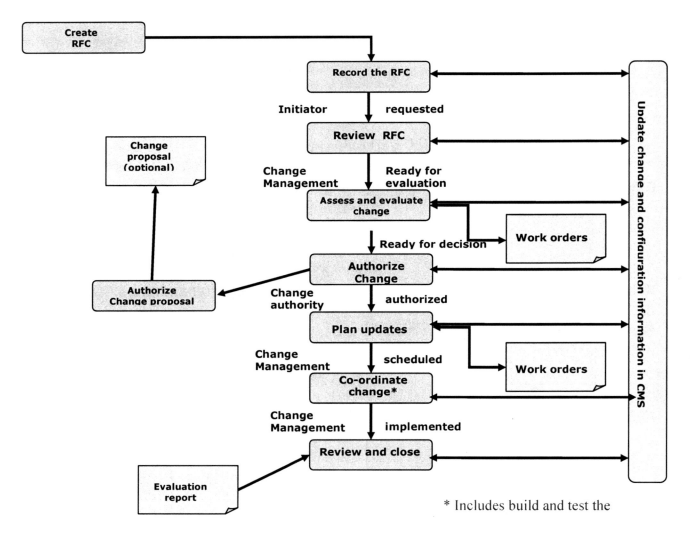

Figure 6.C– The Activities of Change Management

Important Steps:

1. The RFC is logged:
2. An initial review is performed (filter RFCs)
3. The RFCs are assessed – may require involvement of CAB or ECAB.
4. This is authorized by the Change Manager
5. Work orders are issued for the build of the Change (carried out by other groups)
6. Change Management coordinates the work performed.
7. The Change is reviewed.
8. The Change is closed.

Where can RFCs be initiated?

Anywhere (Other ITIL® processes, customers, end-users etc.)

Who does the actual build/test/implement?

- Technical areas
- Project Teams
- Release and Deployment Management

Assessing and Evaluating Changes

To ensure that the Change Management process does not become a bottleneck, it is important to define what Change Models will be used to ensure effective and efficient control and implementation of RFCs.

Impact:	**Escalation Level:**
• Standard	Executed using a pre-defined form/template

Normal Changes

• Minor	Change Manager (CM)
• Significant	Change Advisory Board (CAB)
• Major	IT Management Board

Urgency:

• Normal	Change Manager or CAB
• Emergency	Emergency CAB Committee (ECAB)

The 7Rs of Change Management:

When assessing Changes, it is important to have answers to the following seven questions:

- Who RAISED the change?
- What is the REASON for the change?
- What is the RETURN required from the change?
- What are the RISKS involved in the change?
- What RESOURCES are required to deliver the change?
- Who is RESPONSIBLE for the build, test and implementation of the change?
- What is the RELATIONSHIP between this change and other changes?

These questions must be answered for **all changes**. Without this information the impact assessment cannot be completed, and the balance of risk and benefit to the live service will not be understood. This could result in the change not delivering all the possible or expected business benefits or even of it having a detrimental, unexpected effect on the live service.

Authorization of Changes:

While the responsibility for authorization for Changes lies with the Change Manager, they in turn will ensure they have the approval of three main areas.
- Financial Approval - What's it going to cost? And what's the cost of not doing it?
- Business Approval - What are the consequences to the business? And not doing it?
- Technology Approval - What are the consequences to the infrastructure? And not doing it?

Key Points:
- Consider the implications of performing the Change, as well as the impacts of NOT implementing the Change.
- Importance of empowering Change Manager as their primary role is to protect the integrity of the IT infrastructure.

Relationship with Project Management:

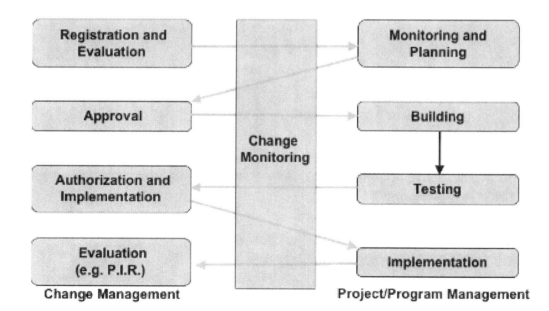

Figure 6.D Relationship with Project Management

How does Change Management work with Project Management?
- Change Management authorizes, controls, coordinates
- ***Does not*** plan, build, test or implement.
- Change Management is concerned with Remediation Planning to ensure that each RFC has a fallback / rollback plan.

Roles and Responsibilities

Change Manager
- Administration of all RFCs.
- Prepare RFCs for CAB meetings, FSC for Service Desk..
- Authorize (or reject) changes.

CAB
- Advises Change Manager on authorization issues for RFCs with significant or major impact.

Release and Deployment Manager
- Manages the release of changes.
- Advises the Change Manager (as part of CAB) on release issues.

Technical specialists
- Build and test the actual change.

Key Performance Indicators (KPIs) of Change Management

It is important that a balanced view of metrics is used when assessing the effectiveness and efficiency of the Change Management process. These metrics include:
- Number of RFCs (Accepted/Rejected)
- Number and % of successful Changes
- Emergency Changes
- Number of Changes awaiting implementation
- Number of implemented Changes
- Change backlogs and bottle-necks
- Business impact of changes
- Frequency of Change to CIs

Challenges affecting Change Management

- Change in culture - 1 central process comes into place that influences everyone's activities
- Bypassing - projects ducking the Change Management planning
- Optimal link with Configuration Management - to execute a controlled change all data MUST be reliable
- Commitment of the supplier(s) to the process
- Commitment of management.

6.3.4 Release and Deployment Management

GOAL: To deploy releases into production and establish effective use of the service in order to deliver value to the customer and be able to handover to Service Operation.

Terminology	Explanations
Release:	A collection of **authorized** Changes to an IT Service.
Release Unit:	A Release Unit describes the portion of a service of IT infrastructure that is normally released together according to the organization's release policy. The unit may vary depending on type(s) or item(s) of service asset or service component such as hardware or software.
Definitive Media Library (DML): *(previously known as the DSL)*	The secure library in which the definitive authorized versions of all media CIs are stored and protected. The DML should include definitive copies of purchased software (along with license documents or information) as well as software developed on site.
Definitive Spares (DS): *(previously known as DHS)*	Physical storage of all *spare IT components and assemblies maintained at the same level as within the live environment.* New IT assemblies are stored here until ready for use, and additional components can be used when needed for additional systems or in the recovery from Incidents. • Details recorded in the CMDB, controlled by Release and Deployment Management.

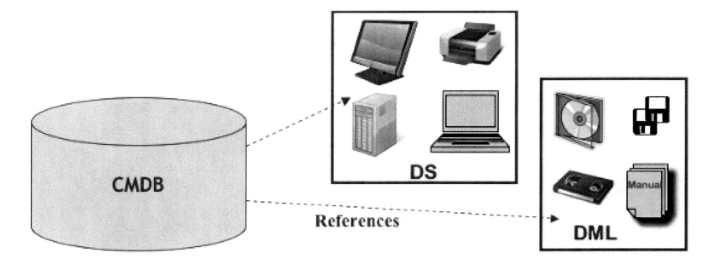

Figure 6.E – The Definitive Media Library and Definitive Spares

Remember – the elements found within the DML and DS are referenced by the CMDB as CIs.

Release and Deployment Management also works closely with Change Management and the Service Desk to inform users of scheduled changes/deployments. Tools used to do this can include:
- email notification
- sms notification,
- verbal communication.

Options for Releases

Big Bang:
The new or changed service is deployed to all user areas in one operation. This will often be used when introducing an application change and consistency of service across the organization is considered important.

The negative aspect of the Big Bang approach is that it increases the risk and impact of a failed Release.

Phased Approach:
The service is deployed to a part of the user base initially, and then this operation is repeated for subsequent parts of the user base via a scheduled rollout plan.

This will be the case in many scenarios such as in retail organizations for new services being introduced into the stores' environment in manageable phases.

The Push Approach:
Is used where the service component is deployed from the centre and pushed out to the target locations.

In terms of service deployment, delivering updated service components to all users, either in big bang or phased form is using the push approach, since the new or changed service is delivered into the users' environment at a time not of their choosing.

The Pull Approach:
Used for software releases where the software is made available in a central location but users are free to pull the software down to their own location at a time of their choosing or when a workstation restarts.

Automated:
The use of technology to automate Releases. This helps to ensure repeatability and consistency. The time required to provide a well-designed and efficient automated mechanism may not always be available or viable.

Manual:
Using manual activities to distribute a Release. It is important to monitor and measure the impact of many repeated manual activities as they are likely to be inefficient and error prone.

Activities

Key Points:

The Release Policy is the overarching strategy for Releases and was derived from the Service Design phase of the Service Lifecycle.

The Release Plan is the operational implementation for each release.

The Rollout Plan is the documented approach for distributing a single Release.

Release Planning:
- Defining the Release contents
- Defining the Release Schedule
- Defining the resources, roles & responsibilities required for the Release.

Design & Test: (Coordinates with other Service Design and Service Transition Processes):
- Produce Release assembly & build instructions
- Create Installation scripts
- Run Test plans
- Develop Back-out procedures
- Produce tested installation procedures

Rollout Planning:
- Defining timetable for distribution
- Identification of affected CIs
- Defining communication plans
- Defining training plans
- Communication & training for:
  - Users
  - Support staff (including the Service Desk)

Logistics, Distribution & Installation:
- Implement the release strategy
- CMDB updated where necessary after installation
- Service Desk is updated about any issues to manage the transition.

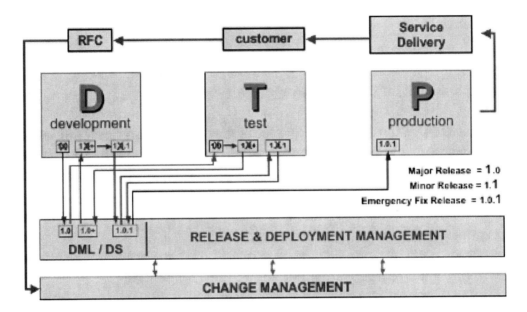

Figure 6.E - Transitioning New and Changed Services into Operation

Note how Change, Release & Deployment, Service Validation & Testing and Service Asset & Configuration Management work together for the transition of new or modified Services.

Roles and Responsibilities

Release & Deployment Manager
- Drive effectiveness & efficiency of process
- Manage release management team
- Liaise with Change & Configuration Management, IT platform managers, Application Developers etc.

Skills: technical & coordination skills, project manager.

Release & Deployment Management Team
- Manage the DML & DS
- Design, build, test & deploy releases.
- Manage software management/distribution tools.

6.3.5 Service Validation and Testing

GOAL: To ensure that new or changed IT Services match the design specification and will meet the needs of the business.

The underlying concept to which Service Validation contributes is quality assurance – establishing that the service design and release will deliver a new or changed service or service offering that is fit for the purpose and fit for use.

Testing is a vital area within Service Management and has often been the unseen underlying cause of what was taken to be inefficient Service Management processes. If services are not tested sufficiently then their introduction into the operational environment will bring rise in:

- **Incidents** – failures in service elements and mismatches between what was wanted and what was delivered impact on business support
- **Service Desk calls for assistance** – services that are not functioning as intended are inherently less intuitive causing higher support requirements
- **Problems and errors** – that are harder to diagnose in the live environment.
- **Costs**, since errors are more expensive to fix in production than if found in testing.
- **Services that are not used effectively** by the users to deliver the desired value.

The Service Validation and Testing process closely collaborates with other Service Transition processes as well as others from across the Service Lifecycle.

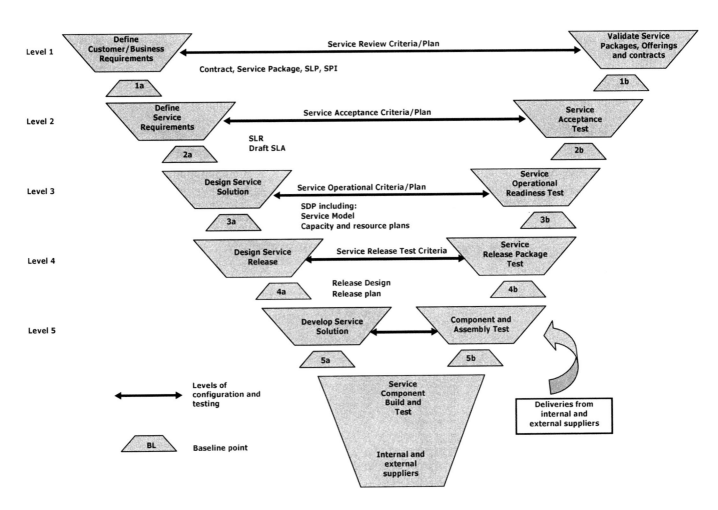

Figure 6.F – The Service V Model

The Service V Model is a concept of establishing acceptance requirements against various levels of requirements that apply in order to **justify release to the customer for trial and assessment.**

The **left hand side** represents the specification of the service requirements down to the detailed Service Design.

The **right hand side** focuses on the validation and test activities that are performed against the specifications defined on the left hand side, and there is direct involvement by the equivalent party on the right hand side.

It shows that service validation and acceptance test planning should start with the definition of service requirements. E.G customers who sign off the agreed service requirements will also sign off the service Acceptance Criteria and test plan if successful.

6.4 Service Transition Summary

Effective Service Transition can significantly improve a Service provider's ability to effectively handle high volumes of change and releases across its Customer base. Other benefits delivered include:

- Increased success rate of Changes and Releases
- More accurate estimations of Service Levels and Warranties
- Less variation of costs against those estimated in budgets
- Less variation from resources plans.

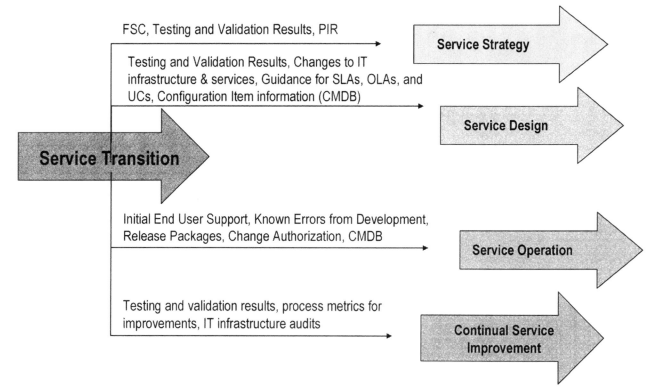

Figure 6.G – Some outputs to other lifecycle phases.

6.5 Service Transition Scenario

Knowledge Management
- If your SKMS is established, you would be able to identify if you have the skills required to support videoconferencing, for example.
- The SKMS will also help to determine the team required to build, test and deploy HYPE.
- User and support documentation

Service Asset and Configuration Management
- HYPE software is registered as CI and relationships between it and the other CIs are known if…when… an incident occurs. This will assist to speed up resolution times.
- Decision made as to whether webcams are CIs themselves or an attribute of the pc/laptop it is attached to

Change Management
- Ensure that the introduction of this new service minimizes impact on other services.. eg – through testing, it is found that the RAM required slows down the pc, affecting other business critical apps. Change Mgt will assist with decision making to determine best path of action (through CAB).

Release and Deployment Management
- Builds and tests HYPE – decision here to limit video resolution to minimize bandwidth.
- Stores original authorized software in DML
- Ensures that design aspects are adhered to when building (eg - ensuring that the password policies are adhered to,
- Organizes training on using HYPE – (inservices Service Desk 1st)

Service Validation and Testing
- Tests HYPE based on customer criteria – (set out in Service Design)
- looks at access, impact on live environment
- As stated previously, found RAM issues and referred back to Change via RFC
- Quality of components

6.6 Service Transition Review Questions

Question 1
Which process would you find the Service V model?
- a) Release Management
- b) Service Transition
- c) Service Validation and Testing
- d) Knowledge Management

Question 2
Release and deployment options include:
1. Big bang vs Phased
2. Automated vs Manual
3. ?
- a) Push vs Proposed
- b) Push vs Pull
- c) Requested vs Forced
- d) Proposed vs Forced

Question 3
The 4 spheres of knowledge management are:
- a) Data, facts, knowledge, wisdom
- b) Ideas, facts knowledge, wisdom
- c) Data, information, facts, wisdom
- d) Data, information, knowledge, wisdom

Question 4
Which activity in Service Asset & Configuration Management would help to ascertain which Configuration Items conform to that which exists in the physical environment?
- a) control
- b) verification and audit
- c) identification
- d) status accounting}

Question 5

After a Change has been implemented, an evaluation is performed. What is this evaluation called?

a) Forward Schedule of Changes (FSC)
b) Post Implementation Review (PIR)
c) Service Improvement Programme (SIP)
d) Service Level Requirement (SLR)

Question 6

Which of the following is not change type?

a) Standard change
b) Normal change
c) Quick change
d) Emergency change

Question 7

Which process is responsible for maintaining the DML?

a) Release and Deployment Management
b) Service asset and configuration Management
c) Service validation and testing
d) Change Management

Question 8

Which process or function is responsible for communicating the forward schedule of changes to the users?

a) Change Management
b) Service Desk
c) Release and Deployment Management
d) Service Level Management

Question 9

Which of the following best describes a baseline?

a) Used as a reference point for later comparison
b) The starting point of any project
c) The end point of any project
d) A rollback procedure

Question 10

The main objective of Change Management is to?
   a) Ensure that any changes are approved and recorded
   b) Ensure that standardised methods and procedures are used for controlled handling of all changes
   c) Ensure that any change requests are managed through the CAB
   d) Ensure that the CAB takes responsibility for all change implementation

7 SERVICE OPERATION

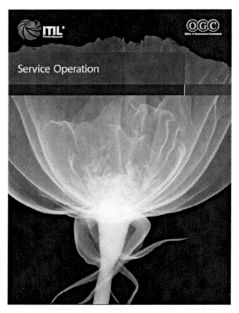

From a customer viewpoint, Service Operation (SO) is where actual value is seen.

This is because it is the execution of strategies, designs and plans and improvements from the Service Lifecycle phases.

Functions	Processes
Service Desk	Incident Management
Technical Management	Problem Management
Application Management	Event Management
IT Operations Management	Request Fulfillment
	Access Management

The Service Operation phase is also concerned with the operational activities that need to be performed for the processes found in the other lifecycle phases.

7.1 Objectives

To enable effectiveness and efficiency in delivery and support of IT services.

Other objectives include:
- Delivering cost-effective stability in the IT infrastructure
- Providing effective and efficient mechanisms to deal with Service Requests, Events, Incidents and Problems.

7.2 Major Concepts

Achieving the Balance

Service Operation is more than just a repetitive execution of a standard set of procedures or activities. SO works in an ever changing environment. This forms a conflict between maintaining the status quo and adapting to changes in the business and technological environments.

One of Service Operation's key roles is to deal with this conflict and to achieve a balance between conflicting sets of priorities.
Error!

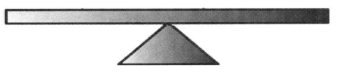

Achieving the Balance

Internal IT View:		External Business View:
Focuses on the way in which IT components and systems are managed to deliver the services.		Focuses on the way in which services are experienced by its users and customers.
An organization here is out of balance and is in danger of not meeting business requirements.	**VS**	An organization has business focus, but tends to under-deliver on promises to the business.
Stability:		Responsiveness:
No matter how good the functionality is of an IT service or how well it has been designed, it will be worth far less if the service components are not available or if they perform inconsistently. Service Operation has to ensure that the IT infrastructure is stable and available as required.	**VS**	Service Operation must recognize that the business and IT requirements change.
However an extreme focus on stability means that IT is in danger of ignoring changing business requirements		When there is an extreme focus on responsiveness IT may tend to overspend on change and also decrease the stability of the infrastructure.

Cost of Service:		Quality of Service:
An organization with an extreme focus on cost is out of balance and is in danger of losing service quality because of heavy cost cutting. The loss of service quality leads to a loss of customers, which in turn leads to further cost cutting as the negative cycle continues.	**VS**	An organization with an extreme focus on quality has happy customers but may tend to overspend to deliver higher levels of service than are strictly necessary, resulting in higher costs and effort required. The goal should be to consistently to deliver the agreed level of IT service to its customer and users, while at the same time keeping costs and resource utilization at an optimal level.
Reactive:		Proactive:
An organization that is extremely reactive is not able to effectively support the business strategy. Unfortunately a lot of organizations focus on reactive management as the sole means to ensure services are highly consistent and stable, actively discouraging proactive behavior from staff. The worst aspect of this approach is that discouraging effort investment in proactive Service Management can ultimately increase the effort and cost of reactive activities and further risk stability and consistency in services.	**VS**	An extremely proactive organization tends to fix services that are not broken, or introduce services that are not yet needed, resulting in higher levels of change, costs and effort. This also comes at a cost of stability to the infrastructure and quality of service already being delivered.

7.3 Service Operation Functions

"Know your role, do your job"

Team motto describing the goal for every player, coach and general staff member of the Kansas City Chiefs.

Functions refer to the people and automated measures that execute a defined process, an activity or combination of both. The functions within Service Operation are needed to manage the 'steady state' operation IT environment. Just like in sports where each player will have a specific role to play in the overall team strategy, IT Functions define the different roles and responsibilities required for the overall Service Delivery and Support of IT Services.

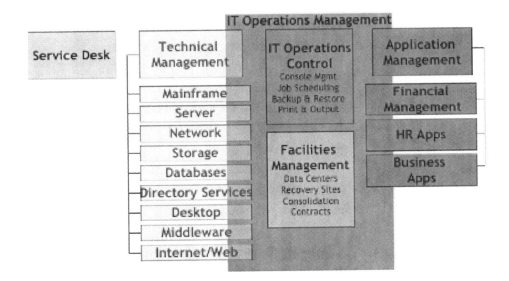

Figure 7.A – The ITIL® Functions from Service Operation

NOTE: These are logical functions and do not necessarily have to be performed by equivalent organizational structure. This means that Technical and Application Management can be organized in any combination and into any number of departments. The lower groupings (eg. Mainframe, Server) are examples of activities performed by Technical Management and are not a suggested organizational structure.

7.3.1 The Service Desk

GOAL: To support the agreed IT service provision by ensuring the accessibility and availability of the IT organization and by performing various supporting activities.

Terminology	Explanation
Service Desk Types:	• *Relates to the skill level and first-time resolution rate for service calls.*
Call Centre:	• *Handling/logging of large volumes of calls. Low first-time resolution rate for calls and requests.*
Help Desk:	• *Manage and co-ordinate incidents. Medium first-time resolution rate for calls and requests.*
Service Desk:	• *A wide variety of services offered. High first-time resolution rate for calls and requests.*
Service Desk Structure:	• *Relates to the physical organization of the service desk.*
Local	• *The Service Desk is situated in the same physical location (or time zone for international organizations) as the user groups that it serves.*
Central	• *A centralized Service Desk serves multiple user groups from different physical locations.*
Virtual	• *A Service Desk that has no physical structure, but instead relies on technology to coordinate call resolution across disparate Service Desk staff and to provide a centralized Knowledgebase.*
Follow-the-Sun	• *Utilizing multiple Service Desks across different time-zones in order to provide 24x7 availability of the Service Desk. Typically there will still be a centrally managed Knowledgebase to enhance the quality of support delivered.*

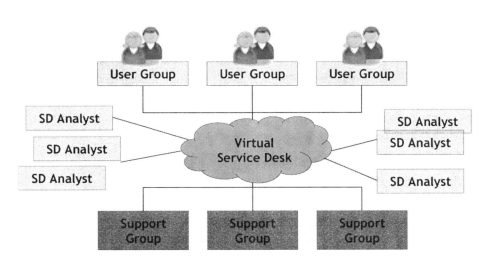

Figure 7.B – A Virtual Service Desk structure

Skills
Due to the role played by the Service Desk, staff members need to have (or have the ability to develop):
- Communication Skills
- Technical Skills
- Business Understanding

The most important of these three are communication skills as the primary role of the Service Desk is to provide a Single Point of Contact between the end-users and the IT organization. Because of this, they will need to be able to deal effectively with a wide-range of people and situations.

Self-Help
Many organizations find it beneficial to offer "Self Help" capabilities to their users. The technology should therefore support this capability with some form of web front-end allowing web pages to be defined offering a menu-driven range of self help and service requests – with a direct interface into the back-end process-handling software. This reduces the amount of calls into the Service Desk and is often used as a source for improvements to efficiency. An example of this is the ability for a customer to track online the status of their parcels when shipped through a major courier company.

Aside from this, the Service Desk will use many different tools, systems and other technology components in order to provide effective and efficient support to end-user calls and requests. To enable this, typical technology components utilized include:
- Computerized service desk systems
- Voice services (adv. menu systems, voicemail, SMS)
- Web and email (access, notification, updates)
- Systems that contain linkages to SLAs, CMDB
- Access to availability monitoring tools
- Self help for customers using technology.

Key Performance Indicators for the Service Desk:
It is important to use a balanced range of metrics for measuring the effectiveness and efficiency of the Service Desk. Typical metrics include:
- Number of calls to Service Desk
- Number of calls to other support staff (look to decrease escalations over time)
- Call resolution time
- Customer satisfaction (surveys)
- Use of self help (where exists)

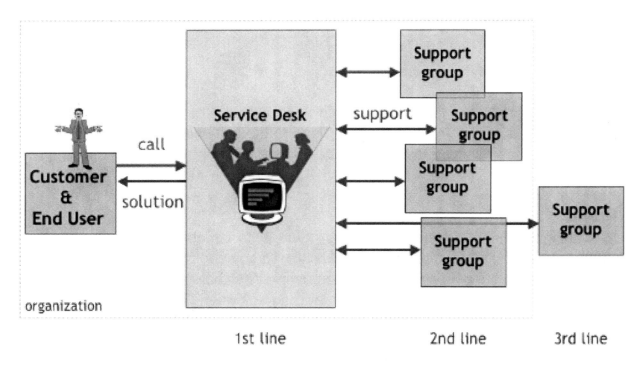

Figure 7.C – The Service Desk managing all end-user communication

7.3.2 Technical Management

Goal: To help plan, implement and maintain a stable technical infrastructure to support the organization's business processes through:
- Well designed and highly resilient, cost effective topology
- The use of adequate technical skills to maintain the technical infrastructure in optimum condition
- Swift use of technical skills to speedily diagnose and resolve any technical failures that do occur.

One or more technical support teams or departments will be needed to provide Technical Management and support for the IT Infrastructure.

In all but the smallest organizations where a single combined team or department may suffice, separate teams or departments will be needed for each type of infrastructure being used. In many organizations the Technical Management (TM) departments are also responsible for the daily operation of a subset of the IT Infrastructure.

In many organizations, the actual role played by IT Operations Management is carried out by either Technical or Application Management.

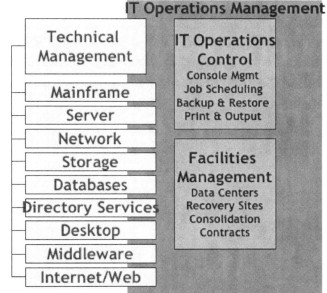

Roles and Responsibilities:
- Custodian of technical knowledge and expertise related to managing the IT Infrastructure. Provides detailed technical skills and resources needed to support the ongoing operation of the IT Infrastructure.
- Plays an important role in providing the actual resources to support the IT Service Management lifecycle. Ensures resources are effectively trained and deployed to design, build, transition, operate and improve the technology to deliver and support IT Services.

  Technical
Management

Specialist Technical
Architects & Designers

Specialist Maintenance
& Support Staff

*(Primarily involved in
Service Operation)*

Figure 7.D – Staff making up the Technical Management Function

It is important that the Technical Management function is made up of both the support staff as well as those involved in the design of the service. This is because quality support needs the input of the design team, and quality design needs input from those who will be supporting the service.

7.3.3 IT Operations Management

Goal: To perform the daily operational activities needed to manage the IT Infrastructure. This is done according to the performance standards defined during Service Design.

In many senses, the function performs many of the logistical activities required for the effective and efficient delivery and support of services (e.g. Event Management).

In some organizations this is a single, centralized department. While in others some activities and staff are centralized and some are provided by distributed and specialized departments.

In many cases, the role of IT Operations Management is actually performed by the Technical and Application Management functions where required.

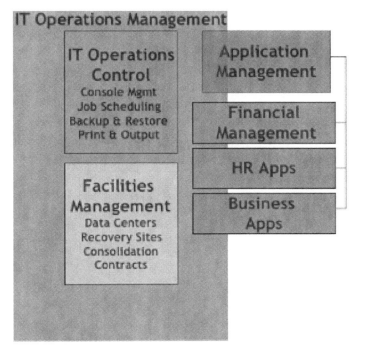

Roles and Responsibilities:
- Maintenance of the 'status quo' to achieve stability of the organization's day to day processes and activities.
- Regular scrutiny and improvements to achieve improved service at reduced costs, whilst maintaining stability.
- Swift application of operational skills to diagnose and resolve any IT operations failures that occur.

IT Operations Management has two unique functions, which are usually organized into two groups:

IT Operations Control: generally staffed by shifts of operators and ensures that routine operational tasks are carried out. Also provides centralized monitoring and control activities, usually using an Operations Bridge or Network Operations Centre. *Event Management* is a process carried out by IT Operations Control.

Facilities Management: management of the physical IT environment, usually data centers or computer rooms. In some organizations many physical components have been outsourced and Facilities Management may include the management of the outsourcing contracts.

7.3.4 Application Management

Goal: To help design, implement and maintain stable applications to support the organization's business processes.

Application Management is usually divided into departments based on the application portfolio of the organization allowing easier specialization and more focused support.

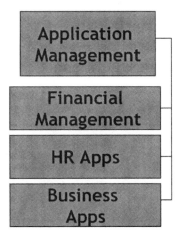

Roles and Responsibilities:
- Managing Applications throughout their lifecycle.
- Supports and maintains operational applications, and plays an important role in design, testing and improvement of applications that form part of IT Services.
- Support the organization's business processes by helping to identify functional and manageability requirements for application software.
- Assist in the design and/or deployment of those applications.
- Provide ongoing support and improvement of those applications.
- Identify skills required to support the applications

7.4 Service Operation Processes

The goal of Service Operation as previously mentioned is to enable effectiveness and efficiency in delivery and support of IT services. The processes that support this goal are:
- Event Management
- Incident Management
- Problem Management
- Request Fulfillment
- Access Management

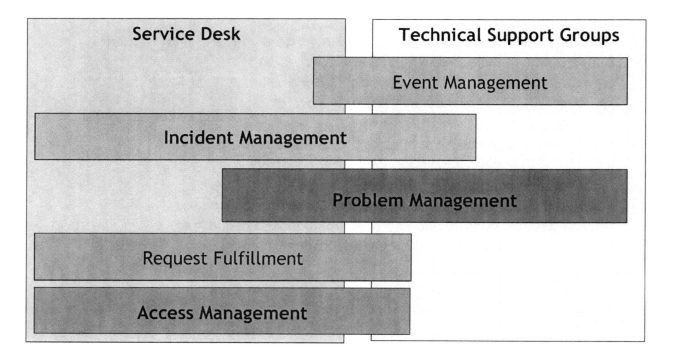

Figure 7.E – Where the Service Operation Processes get carried out

The figure above demonstrates how much responsibility the Service Desk and the Technical Support Groups (Technical, IT Operations and Application Management functions) have in the Service Operation Processes. Incident Management, Request Fulfillment and Access Management are primarily carried out by the Service Desk, with Event Management and Problem Management as primarily 'back-of-house' processes.

7.4.1 Event Management

Goal: To enable stability in IT Services Delivery and Support by monitoring all events that occur throughout the IT infrastructure to allow for normal service operation and to detect and escalate exceptions.

Event Management also:
- Provides the entry point for the execution of many Service Operation processes and activities (e.g. Incident Management)
- Provides a way of comparing actual performance and behaviour against design standards and Service Level Agreements.
- Provides a basis for Service Assurance and Reporting and Service Improvement in the Continual Service Improvement phase.

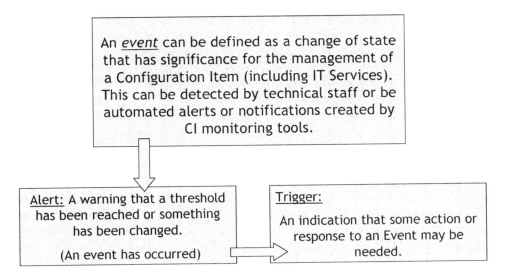

There are many different types of events, for example:

- Events that signify regular operation: *(e.g. A scheduled backup occurred successfully)*

- Events that signify an exception: *(e.g. A scheduled backup failed)*

- Events that signify unusual but not exceptional operation. These are an indication that the situation may require closer monitoring.   *(e.g. No backup initiated within last 72 hours)*

Activities

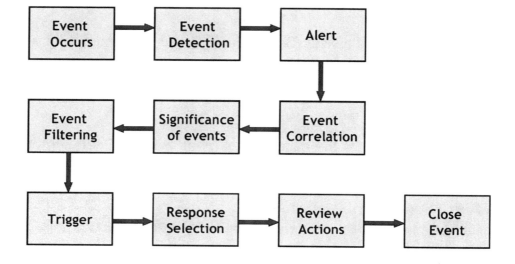

Figure 7.F – Activities of Event Management

NOTE: In most organization's IT infrastructure there would be a significant amount of events occurring every day, which may impact on the way in which events are correlated and provide triggers indicating a response is needed.

7.4.2 Incident Management

Goal: To restore normal service operation *as quickly as possible* and minimize the adverse impact on business operations, thus ensuring that the best possible levels of service quality and availability are maintained.

What is the difference between Incident Management and Problem Management?

Question?
If we had our gardens and lawns being affected by weeds, how would we address the situation?

Incident Management: Use techniques that address the symptoms but still allow the weeds to grow back: (e.g. Pull them out, mow over them, use a hedge-trimmer, and buy a goat).

Problem Management: Use techniques that address the root-cause of the symptoms, so that weeds will no longer grow. (E.g. Use poison, dig roots out, re-lawn, concrete over etc.)

This shows the difference between Incident Management and Problem Management. Incident Management is not concerned with the root cause, only addresses the symptoms as quickly as possible.

What is an Incident?
1) An unplanned interruption to an IT service **or** reduction in the quality of an IT service.
2) Failure of a CI that has not yet affected service, but could likely disrupt service if left unchecked. This can be raised by internal IT staff.

Major Concepts:

Escalation:

Hierarchical

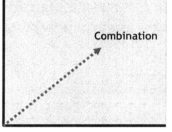

Figure 7.G – Escalation Graph

Escalation is the **human element of Incident Prioritization**. It helps us identify incidents that may need to be moved up or down the priority list due to changing factors or priorities. Escalations can also be combined.

Functional:
- Based on *knowledge or expertise*
- Also known as "Horizontal Escalation"

Hierarchical:
- For corrective actions by authorized *line management*
- Also known as "Vertical Escalation"
- When resolution of an incident will not be in time or satisfactory.

Categorization:

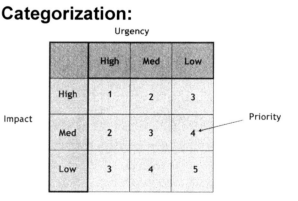

Figure 7.H – Priority Grid

Categorization is the **unemotional/statistical** aspect of prioritization. It uses the following formula:

IMPACT + URGENCY = PRIORITY
- **Impact:** Degree to which the **user/business** is affected
- **Urgency:** Degree to which **resolution** can be delayed

Activities:

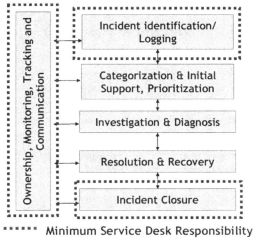

Figure 7.I – Activities of Incident Management

Ownership, Monitoring, Tracking & Communication
- Service Desk OWNS/accountable for ALL Incidents
- Monitor progress, escalation of Incidents
- Advise user and IT management

Incident identification and Logging
- Update/confirm Incident and user details

Categorization, Initial Support, Prioritization (Most critical activity)
- Categorize so the exact type of call is recorded e.g. Incident (Eg. Desktop, Network, Email)
- Assess urgency and impact to assign priority
- Match against existing Problems/Known Errors
- Match multiple Incidents and create new Problem record.
- Prioritization: taking into account the impact and urgency (how quickly to incident needs a resolution).

Investigation and Diagnosis
- Assess the Incident details and provide workaround (if available)
- Escalate to support areas (Functional) or IT management (Hierarchical)

Resolution and Recovery
- Resolve the Incident or raise a RFC

Incident Closure
- Update details of actions taken and classification of Incident.
- Confirm closure with User

Major Incidents

The highest category or impact defined for an incident. A major incident results in significant disruption to the business.

A separate procedure, with shorter timescales and greater urgency, must be used for 'major' incidents. A definition of what constitutes a major incident must be agreed and ideally mapped on to the overall incident prioritization system – such that they will be dealt with through the major incident process. This often leads directly into Problem Management, to ensure that the root-cause of the Incident is removed and the incident never occurs again.

Roles and Responsibilities

Incident Manager:
- Drive effectiveness & efficiency of process
- Manage incident management team
- Ensure SLA targets for Incident resolution are met.

Skills: analytical, technical, business understanding, communication, calm under pressure.

Service Desk:
- Log/record Incidents
- Incident classification and categorization
- Provide initial support
- Match to existing Incident or Problem records
- Manage communication with end-users

1st, 2nd, 3rd line support groups (including Technical and Application Management):
- Incident classification
- Investigation and resolution of Incidents

Key Performance Indicators for Incident Management

Just like any other ITIL® process, a balanced range of metrics must be used to demonstrate effectiveness and efficiency of the Incident Management process, including:

- Total number of incidents
- Percentage of Incidents handled within agreed response time (Incident response-time targets may be specified in SLAs, for example, by impact code)
- Average cost per Incident
- Percentage of Incidents closed by the Service Desk without reference to other levels of support
- Number and percentage of Incidents resolved remotely, without the need for a visit.

Challenges affecting Incident Management:

- Are all calls registered? Under a unique number?
- Which priority codes do we use and how is the priority determined?
- Organization of the 1st line
- Organization of the 2nd line
- What % "closed on first call" is possible through Incident Management?

7.4.3 Problem Management

Goal: To minimize the adverse impact of Incidents and Problems on the business that are caused by errors within the IT infrastructure, and to prevent the recurrence of Incidents related to these errors.

Defined as two major processes:
Reactive Problem Management
Proactive Problem Management **

** (initiated in Service Operation but generally driven as part of Continual Service Improvement)

Remember the weeding analogy used for Incident Management. Problem Management seeks to identify and remove the root-cause of Incidents in the IT Infrastructure.

Terminology	Explanations
Problem:	**Unknown** underlying cause of one or more Incidents (The investigation)
Known Error:	**Known** underlying cause. Successful diagnosis of the root cause of a Problem, and workaround or permanent solution has been identified
KEDB:	Known Error Database, where Known Errors and their documented workarounds are maintained. This database is owned by Problem Management.
Workaround:	The documented technique in which to provide the user with the required functionality, by either alternate means or by carrying out some action required to restore service.

Relationship with other Processes:

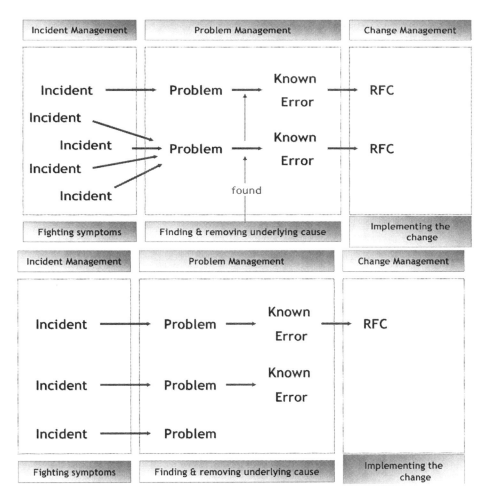

As shown above, the way in which Problems identified and corrected occur in multiple ways. For most organizations, the primary benefit of Problem Management is demonstrated in the "Many to One" relationship between Incidents and Problems. This enables an IT Service Provider to resolve many Incidents in an efficient manner by correcting the underlying root-cause.

Why do some Problems not get diagnosed?
- Because the root cause is not always found.

Why do some Known Errors not get fixed?
- Because we may decide that the costs exceed the benefits of fixing the error or
- Because it may be fixed in an upcoming patch from a Supplier, eg Windows patch or update.

Two Sub-Processes of Problem Management

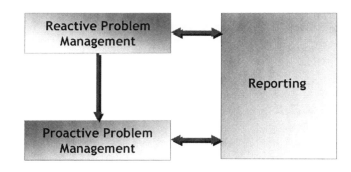

Figure 7.J – The two sub-processes of Problem Management

The activities of Problem Management are carried out within the Proactive and Reactive Problem Management. The main goal of Proactive Problem Management is to identify errors that might otherwise be missed. Proactive Problem Management analyses Incident Records, and uses data collected by other IT Service Management processes and external sources to identify trends or significant problems.

Reactive Problem Management

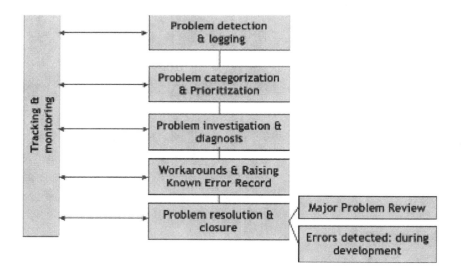

Figure 7.K – The activities of Reactive Problem Management

The activities of Reactive Problem Management are similar to those of Incident Management for the logging, categorization and classification for Problems. The subsequent activities are different as this is where the actual root-cause analysis is performed and the Known Error corrected.

Major Problem Review

After every major problem, while memories are still fresh a review should be conducted to learn any lessons for the future. Specifically the review should examine:

- Those things that were done correctly
- Those things that were done wrong
- What could be done better in the future?
- How to prevent recurrence
- Whether there has been any third-party responsibility and whether follow-up actions are needed.

Such reviews can be used as part of training and awareness activities for staff – any lessons learned should be documented in appropriate procedures, working instructions, diagnostic scripts or Known Error Records.

Proactive Problem Management

The two main activities of Proactive Problem Management are:

- **Performing a Trend Analysis**
  - Review reports from other processes (e.g. Incident, Availability Management)
  - Identify recurring Problems or training opportunities.
- **Targeting Preventative Action**
  - Perform a cost - benefit analysis of all costs associated with prevention
  - Target specific areas taking up the most support attention

Roles and Responsibilities

Problem Manager

- Drive effectiveness & efficiency of process
- Manage the Problem Management team
- Liaise with customers, IT executive, IT platform managers

Skills:

- Business knowledge,
- Lateral thinker, coordination skills.

Problem Management Team (including Application and Technical Management functions)

- Reactive & proactive problem management
- Provide management reports
- Assist Incident Management

Skills:

- Analytical, technical, business knowledge

7.4.4 Request Fulfilment

Goal: To provide an effective and efficient channel for users to make requests, gain information and obtain standard Services.

A Service Request is:
- A request for information or advice
- A request for a *standard* change
- A request for access to an IT Service

Standard Change: Eg. User asking for a password reset or for the provision of standard IT services. These are usually handled by the Service Desk and do get implemented via the normal steps of Change Management.

Roles and Responsibilities:
Request Fulfilment is primarily carried out by the Service Desk Function, but is also assisted by other teams within the IT organization.

Just like Change Management, to assist with Request Fulfilment many organizations will wish to create pre-defined Request Models. These would typically include some form of pre-approval by Change Management.

7.4.5 Access Management

Goal: To *grant* authorized users the right to use a Service while *preventing* access to non-authorized users in order to protect the confidentiality, integrity and availability (CIA) of information and infrastructure.

Relationship with other Processes

Access Management is the execution of policies and actions defined in Information Security and Availability Management.

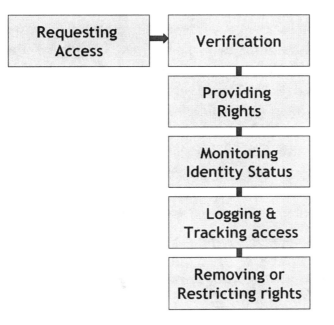

Figure 7.L – Access Management Activities

Figure 7.L demonstrates the lifecycle for managing access to services, information and facilities.

7.5 Service Operation Summary

From a customer viewpoint, Service Operation is where actual value is seen. This is because it is the execution of strategies, designs and plans and improvements from the Service Lifecycle phases.

Key benefits delivered as a result of Service Operation are:
- Effectiveness and efficiency in IT Service delivery and support
- Increased return on investment

Other benefits can be defined as:
1. **Long term:** Over a period of time the Service Operation processes, functions performance and output are evaluated. These reports will be analyzed and decisions made about whether the improvement is needed, and how best to implement it through Service Design and Transition. e.g. deployment of new tools, changes to process designs, reconfiguration of the infrastructure.

2. **Short term:** improvement of working practices within the Service Operations processes, functions and technology itself. Generally they involve smaller improvements that do not mean changes to the fundamental nature of a process or technology. E.g. tuning, training, personnel redeployment etc.

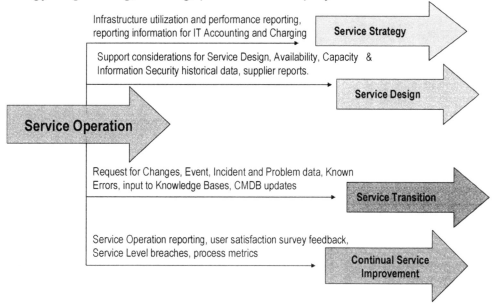

Figure 7.M – Some outputs to other lifecycle phases.

7.6 Service Operation Scenario

Functions

Service Desk
- Service desk has been trained in HYPE and can support users.
- Has access to known errors and workarounds to resolve incidents

Technical Management
- Designed, built, tested and rolled HYPE out into live environment
- Supports HYPE service

Application Management
- Made modifications to HYPE application to ensure effectively interfaced with XY app.
- Provided training on HYPE to users and Service Desk

IT Operations Management
- creates backups of logs, monitors component events

Processes

Event Management
- sends alerts to IT Ops when HYPE logs backups pass/fail
- monitors thresholds for triggers on bandwidth (set up in Availability Management)

Request Fulfilment Management
- users use this process to request copy of logs

Access Management
- password reset of HYPE account – provide authorized users access

Incident Management and Problem Management will not be discussed in this example.

7.7 Service Operation Review Questions

Question 1
What is the best definition of an Incident Model?
 a) Predicting the impact of incidents on the network
 b) A type of Incident that is used as a best practice model
 c) A set of pre-defined steps to be followed when dealing with a known type of Incident
 d) An Incident that requires a separate system

Question 2
What is the difference between a Known Error and a Problem?
 a) The underlying cause of a Known Error is known. The underlying cause of a Problem is not known
 b) A Known Error involves an error in the IT infrastructure, A Problem does not involve such an error.
 c) A Known Error always originates from an Incident. This is not always the case with a Problem.
 d) With a Problem, the relevant Configuration Items have been identified. This is not the case with a Known Error.

Question 3
Information is regularly exchanged between Problem Management and Change Management. What information is this?
 a) Known Errors from Problem Management, on the basis of which Change Management can generate Requests for Change (RFCs)
 b) RFCs resulting from Known Errors
 c) RFCs from the users that Problem Management passes on to Change Management
 d) RFCs from the Service Desk that Problem Management passes on to Change Management

Question 4
Incident Management has a value to the business by?
 a) Helping to control cost of fixing technology
 b) Enabling customers to resolve Problems
 c) Helping to maximise business impact
 d) Contributing to the reduction of impact

Question 5

Which of the following is NOT an example of a Service Request?

a) A user calls the Service Desk to order a new mouse
b) A user calls the Service Desk because they would like to change the functionality of an application
c) A user calls the service desk to reset their password
d) A user logs onto an internal web site to download a licensed copy of software from a list of approved options

Question 6

The BEST definition of an event is?

a) A situation where a capacity threshold has been exceeded and an agreed Service Level has already been impacted
b) An occurrence that is significant for the management of the IT Infrastructure or delivery of services
c) A problem that requires immediate attention
d) A social gathering of IT staff to celebrate the release of a service

Question 7

Technical Management is NOT responsible for?

a) Maintenance of the local network
b) Identifying technical skills required to manage and support the IT Infrastructure
c) Defining the Service agreements for the technical infrastructure
d) Response to the disruption to the technical infrastructure

Question 8

Which of the following is NOT an objective of Service Operation?

a) Through testing, to ensure that services are designed to meet business needs
b) To deliver and support IT Services
c) To manage the technology used to deliver services
d) To monitor the performance of technology and processes

Question 9

Which of the following BEST describes the purpose of Event Management?

a) The ability to detect events, analyse them and determine the appropriate control action
b) The ability to coordinate changes in events
c) The ability to monitor and control projected service outages
d) The ability to report on success of all batch processing jobs

Question 10

Which process or function is responsible for management of the Data centre facility?

    a) IT Operations Control
    b) Supplier Management
    c) Facilities Management
    d) Technical Function

8 Continual Service Improvement

Processes:

- Service Level Management*
- Service Measurement & Reporting
- CSI Improvement Process

*Although Service Level Management primarily fits within the Service Design Phase, it plays a very large part in CSI, and therefore is discussed in this section.

8.1 Objectives

To ensure continual improvements to IT Service Management Processes and IT Services.

Continual Service Improvement is the phase that binds all the other elements of the Service Lifecycle together and ensures that both the service and the IT Service Provider continually improves and matures.

8.2 Major Concepts

The Continual Service Improvement Model
The CSI Model provides the basis by which improvements are made to both services and the capabilities of an IT Service Provider. They are questions asked in order to ensure all the required elements are identified to achieve continual improvement.

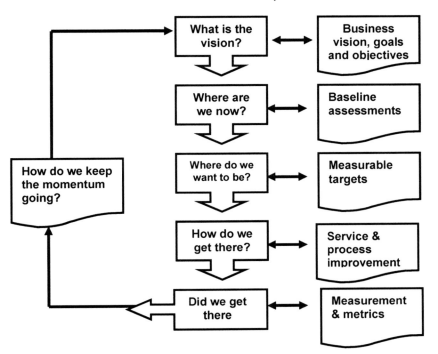

Figure 8.A – Continual Service Improvement Model.

The Continual Service Improvement Model summarizes the constant cycle for improvement. The questions require close interactions with all the other ITIL® processes in order to achieve Continual Service Improvement.

Relationships within the Service Lifecycle:
- **What is the Vision?** Service Strategy, Service Portfolio
- **Where are we now?** Baselines taken using Service Portfolios, Service Level Management, Financial Management for IT etc.
- **Where do we want to be?** Service Portfolio, Service Measurement and Reporting.
- **How do we get there?** CSI and all ITIL® processes!
- **Did we get there?** Service Measurement and Reporting
- **How do we keep the momentum going?** Continual Service Improvement.

8.3 Continual Service Improvement Processes

8.3.1 Service Level Management

GOAL: To ensure that that the levels of IT service delivery are achieved, both for existing services and new services in accordance with the agreed targets.

Service Level Management is a critical element of Continual Service Improvement. Why embark on any service improvement initiative if the customers and the business are satisfied with the levels of service received? Because business requirements change!

Activities

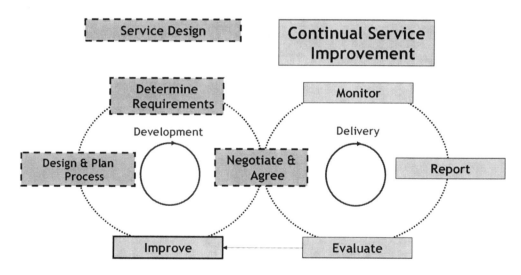

Figure 8.B – The Activities of Service Level Management

Service Level Management (SLM) is a process that is found within two Service Lifecycle phases.

Within Service Design, Service Level Management is concerned with:
- Design and plan the process
- Determining Service Level Requirements (SLRs)
- Negotiating and Agreeing upon SLAs, OLAs and UCs.

Within Continual Service Improvement, Service Level Management is concerned with improving services and processes through constant:
- Monitoring (executed within Service Operation)
- Reporting
- Evaluating
- Improving

The major focus of Service Level Management within Continual Service Improvement is **identifying potential service improvements.**

Service Improvement Plans

Service Improvement Plans are formal plans to implement improvements to a process or service. They are used to ensure that improvement actions are identified and carried out on a regular basis.

The identified improvements may come from:
- breaches of Service Level Agreements
- identification of user training and documentation issues
- weak system testing
- identified weak areas within internal and external support groups.

Roles and Responsibilities

Service Level Manager:
- Must be senior enough to represent organization; with *authority* to do what is necessary
- Manages Service Catalogue, SLAs, UCs, OLAs
- Identifies and manages improvements to services and processes
- Analyses and reports on SL Achievements

Skills:
- Relationship Management
- Patience, tolerance and resilience
- Understanding of the Customer's business and how IT contributes to the delivery of that product or service

Challenges Affecting Service Level Management:

- Monitoring of pre-SLA achievements
- Targets that are achievable
- SLAs based on desire and not achievable targets
- Insufficient focus, resources and time
- Inadequate seniority of SLM staff
- Underpinning contracts ignored
- SLAs too long, not customer focused
- Improvement actions not adhered to

Key Performance Indicators of Service Level Management

Statistics:

- Number/Percentage of services covered by SLAs
- Number/Percentage SLAs supported by UCs & OLAs
- Number/Percentage of service targets being met

Yes/Why Questions:

- Are service level achievements improving?
- Are customer perception statistics improving?
- Are IT costs for service provisions decreasing for services with stable (acceptable but not improving) Service Level Achievements?

Implementing effective and efficient Service Level Management should produce a "Yes" answer to each of the above questions.

If the answer is no:

If the answer is "No" to any of these questions, the very next question that should be asked is "Why?"

From this we can investigate where the process is deficient and begin a plan for improvement. Communicating this to the business also gives them a better understanding of the complexity of providing the services and more importantly allows the business to be actively involved with assessing the costs, risks and plausibility of what will be needed in order to bridge the gap.

8.3.2 Service Measurement and Reporting

GOAL: To coordinate the design of metrics, data collection and reporting activities from the other processes and functions.

There are four main reasons to monitor and measure:

- **Validate**: Are we supporting the strategy and vision?
- **Direct**: Based on factual data, people can be guided to change behaviour
- **Justify**: Do we have the right targets and metrics?
- **Intervene**: Take corrective actions such as identifying improvement opportunities

Measurement of all the process metrics takes place throughout all the Lifecycle phases. CSI uses the results of these measurements to identify and establish improvements via reports.

Types of Metrics:

There are 3 types of metrics that an organization will need to collect to support CSI activities as well as other process activities:

- **Technology Metrics:** often associated with component and application-based metrics such as performance, availability etc

- **Process Metrics:** Captured in the form of KPIs and activity metrics for the service management processes. They help to determine the overall health of a process. 4 key questions KPIs can help answer are centered around quality, performance, value and compliance. CSI uses these metrics to identify improvement opportunities for each process.

- **Service Metrics:** The results of the end-to-end service. Component metrics are used to calculate the service metrics.

Baselines:

A benchmark used as a reference point for later comparison.

It is important that baselines as documents are recognized and accepted throughout the organization. Baseline must be established at each level: strategic goals, and objectives, tactical process maturity and operational metrics and KPIs.

Examples

1. A Service Level Achievement Baseline can be used a starting point to measure the effect of a Service Improvement Plan.
2. A performance Baseline can be used to measure changes in performance over the lifetime of an IT service.
3. A Configuration Management baseline can be used to enable the IT infrastructure to be restored to a known configuration if a change or release fails.

8.3.3 CSI (7 Step) Improvement Process

GOAL: To coordinate a structured approach for improvements to IT services and ITSM processes

The Deming Cycle: A foundation for continual improvement:

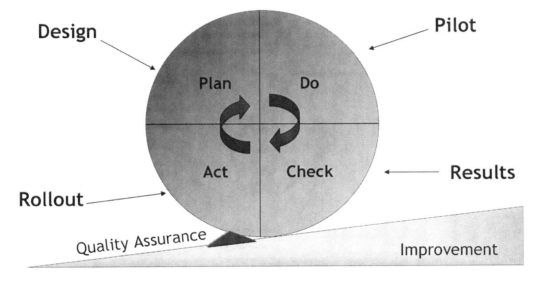

Source: Deming

Figure 8.C – The Deming Cycle

Continuous improvement is a part of every process in ITIL®. The CSI Improvement Process is based on the Deming Cycle of Continual Improvement (Plan, Do, Check, Act)

Implementing ITIL®/ITSM is an ongoing activity, where you improve quality through incremental steps. These four steps are carried out in the exact order, as many times as necessary in order to achieve the improvement desired.

Some of the items that occur during each of the 4 phases:
- **Plan:**   Scope, requirements, objectives, Roles and Responsibilities
- **Do:**   Funds, Policies, reports, managing, changing
- **Check:**   Monitor against plans, survey, report
- **Act:**   Policy on improvement, assess, implement (if appropriate)

Notes on William Edwards Deming:

An American statistician best known for his work in Japan in the post-WWII period. There, from 1950 onward he taught top management how to improve design (and thus service), product quality, testing and sales (the last through global markets). Deming made a significant contribution to Japan's later renown for innovative high-quality products and its economic power.

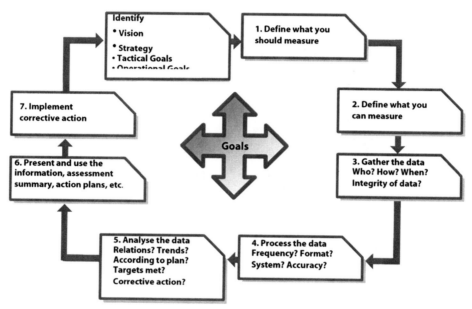

Figure 8.D – The CSI (7 Step) Improvement Process

The Deming Cycle is transformed into more detailed steps and actions to be taken for the improvement of IT services and IT Service Management processes. Like the Deming Cycle, these steps need to be taken in sequential order, as many times as necessary to drive the improvement desired.

8.4 Continual Service Improvement Summary

There is great value to the business when service improvement takes a holistic approach throughout the entire lifecycle. Continual Service Improvement enables this holistic approach to be taken.

Some key benefits of the Continual Service Improvement phase:
- Increased growth
- Competitive Advantage
- Increased Return On Investment
- Increased Value On Investment

ROI: Return on investment – Difference between the benefit (saving) achieved and the amount expended to achieve that benefit, expressed as percentage. Logically we would like to spend a little to save a lot.

VOI: Value on investment – Extra value created by establishment of benefits that include non-monetary or long term outcomes. ROI is a subcomponent of VOI.

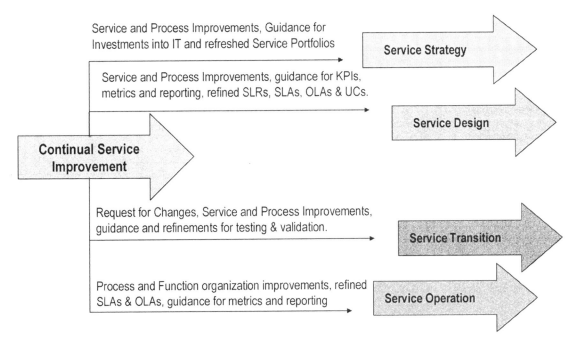

Figure 8.E – Some outputs to other lifecycle phases.

8.5 Continual Service Improvement Scenario

Service Level Management

SLM will be constantly reviewing the SLA and achievements to see if targets are being met. For example – it was found that the availability of the service dropped to 80%. This combined with the increase in the use of the HYPE service, it was decided to implement a Service Improvement Plan(SIP) to identify how this service can be improved.

Service Measurement and Reporting

To do this effectively, it was necessary to take metrics and data and analyze against targets.

CSI Process

The CSI improvement model was used as a roadmap for this SIP. As the business needs changed, so to had their perceived value of HYPE. HYPE had become an integral part of the business communication plan. As a result, new business plans/goals were established and new targets set, with an action plan for improvement… at a cost of course.
This will identify:
- Technology improvements
- Process improvements
- Document improvements
- Training etc

And so it continues!

8.6 Continual Service Improvement Review Questions

Question 1
Why should monitoring and measuring be used when trying to improve services?
   a) To validate, justify, monitor and improve
   b) To validate, direct, justify and intervene
   c) To validate, check, act and improve
   d) To validate, analyse, direct and improve

Question 2
Which is the first activity of the Continual Service Improvement (CSI) model?
   a) Assess the customer's requirements
   b) Understand the vision of the business
   c) Identify what can be measured
   d) Develop a plan for improvement

Question 3
The four stages of the Deming Cycle are?
   a) Plan, Assess, Check, Report
   b) Plan, Do, Check, Act
   c) Plan, Check, Revise, Improve
   d) Plan, Do, Act, Assess

Question 4
Which of the following is NOT a step in the Continual Service Improvement (CSI) model?
   a) What is the vision?
   b) Did we get there?
   c) Who will help us get there?
   d) Where are we now?

Question 5
What is the CORRECT order of the first four activities in the 7 Step Improvement Process?
   a) Define what you should measure, define what you can measure, gather data and process data
   b) Plan, Do, Check, Act
   c) What is the vision, where are we now, where do we want to be, how do we get there?
   d) Gather data, process data, analyse data, present data

9 ITIL® Foundation Exam Tips

Exam Details:

- 40 questions
- The correct answer is only one of the four
- 60 minutes duration
- 26 out of 40 is a pass (65%)
- Closed book
- No notes

Practical Suggestions:

- Read the question CAREFULLY

- At this level of exam the obvious answer is often the correct answer *(if you have read the question carefully!!)*

- Beware of being misled by the preliminary text for the question

- If you think there should be another choice that would be the right answer, then you have to choose the "most right"

- Use strategies such as *"What comes first?"* or *"What doesn't belong?"* to help with the more difficult questions.

Make sure that you prepare adequately in the lead up to your exam by reviewing your notes, reading any available material and attempting the sample exams.

We wish you luck in your exam and future IT Service Management career!

10 Answers

Service Strategy – Pages 30-31

ANSWERS

1c, 2a, 3a, 4c, 5b, 6a, 7d, 8b, 9b, 10d

Service Design – Pages 60-61

ANSWERS

1b, 2c, 3d, 4d, 5b, 6b, 7a, 8b, 9c, 10d

Service Transition-Pages 84-85

ANSWERS

1c, 2b, 3d, 3b, 5b, 6c, 7a, 8b, 9a, 10b

Service Operation – Pages 113-114

ANSWERS

1c, 2a, 3b, 4d, 5b, 6b, 7c, 8a, 9a, 10c

Continual Service Improvement –Pages 125-126

ANSWERS

1b, 2b, 3b, 4c, 5a

11 Glossary

Alert: A warning that a threshold has been reached, something has changed, or a failure has occurred.

Asset: Any resource or capability.

Application Sizing: Determines the hardware or network capacity to support new or modified applications and the predicted workload.

Baselines: A benchmark used as a reference point for later comparison.

CMDB: Configuration Management Database

CMS: Configuration Management System

Configuration Item (CI): Any component that needs to be managed in order to deliver an IT Service.

DML: Definitive Media Library

Function: A team or group of people and the tools they use to carry out one or more processes or activities.

Incident: An unplanned interruption to, or reduction in the quality of, an IT service

Known Error: A problem that has a documented Root Cause and a Workaround

KEDB: Known Error Database

Maintainability: A measure of how quickly and effectively a CI or IT service can be restored to normal after a failure.

Modeling: A technique used to predict the future behavior of a system, process, CI etc

MTBF: Mean Time Between Failures (Uptime)

MTBSI: Mean Time Between Service Incidents

MTRS: Mean Time to Restore Service (Downtime)

OLA: Operational Level Agreement

Process: A structured set of activities designed to accomplish a specific objective.

Process Owner: Role responsible for ensuring that a process is fit for purpose.

Remediation: Recovery to a known state after a failed Change or Release

RFC: Request for Change

Service: A means of delivering value to Customers by facilitating Outcomes Customers want to achieve without the ownership of specific Costs and risks

Service Owner: Role that is accountable for the delivery of a specific IT service

SCD: Supplier and Contracts Database

Service Assets: Any capability or resource of a service provider

Serviceability: Measures Availability, Reliability, Maintainability of IT services/CI's under control of external suppliers.

SIP: Service Improvement Plan

SKMS: Service Knowledge Management System

SLA: Service Level Agreement

SLM: Service Level Manager

SLR: Service Level Requirements

SSIP: Supplier Service Improvement Plan

Status Accounting: Reporting of all current and historical data about each CI throughout its lifecycle.

Trigger An indication that some action or response to an event may be needed.

Tuning: Used to identify areas of the IT infrastructure that could be better utilized.

UC: Underpinning Contract

Utility: Functionality offered by a product or service to meet a particular need. Often summarized as 'what it does'.

VBF: Vital Business Function

Warranty: A promise or guarantee that a product or service will meet its agreed requirements.

12 Certification

12.1 ITIL® Certification Pathways

There are many pathway options that are available to you once you have acquired your ITIL® Foundation Certification. Below illustrates the possible pathways that available to you. Currently it is intended that the highest certification is the ITIL® V3 Expert, considered to be equal to that of Diploma Status.

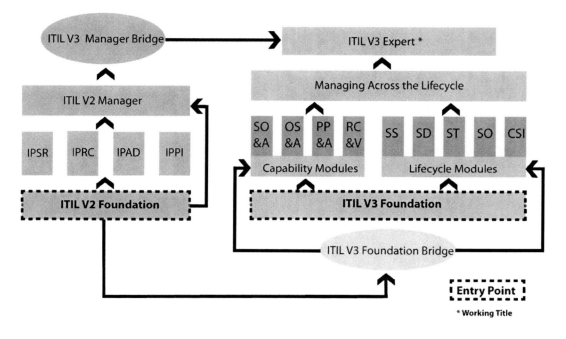

Figure 12.A – ITIL® Certification Pathway

For more information on certification and available programs please visit our website http://theartofservice.com.

12.2 ISO/IEC 20000 Pathways

ISO/IEC 20000 Standard is becoming a basic requirement for IT Service providers and is fast becoming the most recognized symbol of quality regarding IT Service Management processes. Once you have acquired your ITIL® Foundation Certification, you are eligible to pursue the ISO/IEC 20000 certification pathways. ISO/IEC 20000 programs aim to assist IT professionals master and understand the standard itself and issues relating to earning actual standards compliance.

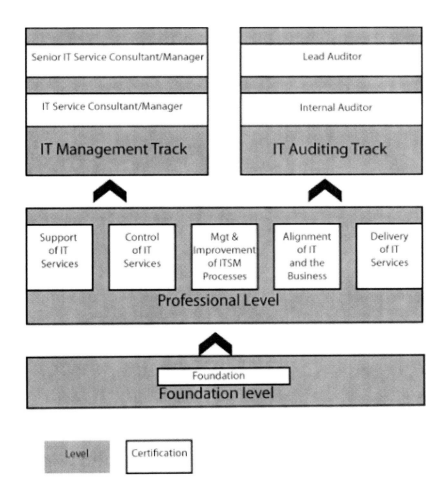

Figure 12.B – ISO/IEC 20000 Certification Pathway

For more information on certification and available programs please visit our website http://theartofservice.com.

Printed in the United States
125510LV00001B/73-176/P